IN SEARCH OF AMY

AMY LANGLEY

Amy Langley

ISBN: 9781695699083

DEDICATION

This book is dedicated to my Mommikins, Nancy Marie Smith Crawford, who encouraged me to write this book. Her words, "Don't die with your book in you," helped me get over my fear. My hope is that you too will overcome your fear and publish your book. The world needs to hear from you Mommy.

Amy Langley

CONTENTS

	Acknowledgments	i
1	Thy Father and Thy Mother	1
2	Leave and Cleave	30
3	Miracles	45
4	Growing Pains	69
5	Letting Go	78
6	Searching for Kate Carter	83
7	His Purpose	95
8	The Truth of the Matter	104
9	F.L.O. For Ladies Only	117

Amy Langley

ACKNOWLEDGMENTS

I have to first thank my loving and understanding husband, Bernard. Not only did he encourage me to keep writing when I wanted to quit, he also tolerated the extra hours that I kept the lights on at night while he was resting. Thank you my love for loving me unconditionally and always seeing the best in me. I love you.

Thank you to my children, Logan and David, who patiently waited for me to finish writing this book so that they could again have my undivided attention. I love you all more than you will ever understand. You are the best parts of me.

A special thanks to Rickia, it was your ambition and drive that kept me motivated. I am forever grateful for our friendship.

Thank you to my editor, Nicole Green. God gave me you. I appreciate you so much.

And I would be remiss if I didn't thank God for it all.

CHAPTER ONE
THY FATHER AND THY MOTHER

"Honor thy father and thy mother: that thy days may be long upon the land which the Lord thy God giveth thee."
Exodus 20:12

Let me introduce myself. I am Amy Nichelle Langley, and I would like to take you on my journey to find me. Things are never as they seem. Since March of 2019, I had been walking around in a fog. My life was normal up until one fateful March night. From that day forward, I had been on an emotional rollercoaster. I've learned that no one is ever what you see on the outside. Often, the complex chapters of a story have been hidden within the story itself. Secrets are plentiful. There is always a story. My parents have their own story, and I would never do them the injustice of trying to tell it. I can't, however, pen mine without including them. My story will introduce you to my mother and father through my eyes from my perspective. I understand that it may not resonate with some, but that's okay. It's my story, and it's about me. It's about seeking and finding. It's about finding Amy.

I wasn't certain of whether to start from the beginning and bring you up-to-date or to start from where I am and work my way backwards. I thought it best if I simply started from my heart. My quest for finding me began at a very early age. It was largely due to not having my biological father in my life. I never talked about my daddy issues but I had them. You see, I grew up with my Mom. She was young, a teenage mother and I was with her through her journey into becoming a woman. We grew up together. At times she made choices that exposed me to things a child should never see nor hear, but her need to do things her way left her no alternatives. In my immature, childlike way, I thought that my fathers' presence would have made life easier, safer and better for my mother and me but that thought never manifested into a reality. I've never experienced a life with my dad. It had always been my mom and I. Together we saw some tough times.

I've agonized at taking this journey for years. I was skeptical about writing it because writing left me no choice but to be transparent and vulnerable and worst of all, I would have to be honest. Recent revelations have ignited my desire to write. Penning this story has made me relive moments that I wanted to be bad dreams or even figments of my imagination and not reality. I needed some peace but I knew that peace came with truth and sometimes truth hurts. I would have to tell the truth. The truth shall set you free, right? Well, here it is here is my truth. For years I didn't like my mother. At one point in my life, I've even hated her. There I said it. It's taken forty-eight years to tell that truth. I didn't like my own mother.

A considerable portion of my life has been spent trying to win my mothers approval and acceptance. I hated the feeling of rejection that had become commonplace in our relationship. When I gave my life to Christ, I looked to her for approval. I thought that she would see me in a different light. When I got married, I looked for her approval. I even looked for her approval when I became a parent. For the most part, she did approve of who I had become as an adult so saying I didn't like her is hard and even confusing for me. My admittance is probably the most transparent I've ever been and will ever be when it comes to my mother. Those who know both, my mother and I, may find it hard to digest. My mother and I have, over the years, become quite the thespians. We've put on Oscar winning performances before our audiences. I love my Mother dearly. As a matter a fact, I love her on a level that's hard to explain, but sometimes I just don't like her. Sounds like an oxymoron, right? Hopefully, you will understand as you go on this journey with me or perhaps you won't. Either way it's my truth.

My mother is a beautiful woman. As a child, I used to watch her as she meticulously applied her makeup whenever she left the house for work or play. She isn't your stereotypical beauty. She doesn't have long hair cascading down her back. She is not built like Kim Kardashian or Beyonce, although in her youth she probably could have given them both some serious competition. No, she is just a beautiful woman, an everyday naturally beautiful woman.

She has beautiful skin, wide hips and the perfect shape and size lips. Her imperfections only enhanced her beauty. My friends always comment on how beautiful she is, and I've witnessed more than enough potential suitors vying for her attention.

My mom isn't only beautiful; she's also giving and intelligent. She has a heart of gold. She has opened her home to countless friends and family who were in need of a place to stay. She would give a stranger her last dime. Her charitable ways sometimes went too far and oftentimes when she found herself needing help, she would be hard pressed to find the same kind gestures she so often extended to others. This however, never deterred her from extending help whenever and wherever she could. She's smart in a worldly kind of way. She soaks up everything she reads and she reads a lot. She's very complex. She loves jazz, art, and is very passionate about the plight of our people. She loves to read and she loves to write. I guess that's where I got my love for reading and writing. Despite all of her beauty, kindness and intellect, there is another side of her that in many cases has made her ugly to me. I told you, she is complex. When I was younger, I thought she was mean.

I guess I should go back to the beginning to help you understand. I was born to a teenage mother. She was a naive sixteen-year-old when I was conceived and seventeen years old when I was born. She had her own mommy issues. She longed to throw in the hand that life had dealt her. She became smitten with a young man from the neighborhood who also had the eyes of other young ladies in the neighborhood. She was in love with him, they had sex, and nine months later, on Thanksgiving Day, I was born. Ironically, I'm not sure how thankful anyone was about my conception or birth. My mother once told me that when she presented him with the news of her pregnancy, he questioned the paternity. I think at the time, my mother may have loved my father and the thought of having his child, more than she actually loved me.

My father's absence from my life had a significant impact. He was what you would call a "street" dude or perhaps a "bad boy" and even did time in jail, and yet my mother never had a bad word to say about him or to him. It didn't matter that he had never contributed financially towards my upbringing. She never threatened him with child support, and she never complained about his neglect. She wasn't the angry or vengeful "baby mama" that we sometimes hear about today.

There are no pictures of my father holding me as a baby. I have no recollection of him looking into my eyes or holding me when I was a child. I've never ridden in a car with him to get ice cream. There were never any stories of him visiting me at the home my mom shared with my grandma and aunt. I can recall no stories that involved him ever having any interaction with me when I was a child. There are no stories and there are no pictures. There were no birthday cards or presents and Christmas was definitely a "no show." All I have are memories of her sharing how smitten she was with him and how much she loved him, her first love. There were no stories of how much he loved me or how much she loved me when I was born- nope, only how much she loved him. He was her first love and yet I was not their love child. Recently, on a road trip from her hometown to D.C., my mom confessed that she still loved and cared for him. I was a little taken aback but I played it cool. I wasn't trying to rehash old feelings that I had decided to let go of a long time ago.

As a child, I believed my mother didn't like me because he didn't choose her. I was the first of his seven children. He married another young lady from my mother's neighborhood and had two sons. It had always been my thought that my mom was hurt and disappointed by his rejection, and took it out on me because I was his child. Maybe seeing me everyday reminded her of the rejection. I wondered often, had she left her small hometown to escape the hurt of him not choosing her.

As a little girl I remember thinking that she really hated me. I mean what mother doesn't have baby pictures of her firstborn? Our homes (we've lived in a gazillion places) were always immaculate and stylish, for my mother has a unique gift for interior decorating. She can turn a cardboard box into the most comfortable and coziest of places. Yet, in all of the beautiful places we've lived, there were never pictures of me as a baby or a toddler, anywhere. Not on the mantles, not on any bookshelves and certainly not on the walls. Hell, there weren't pictures of me as a baby in any of our photo albums. Not only did she not have any pictures, she didn't have any keepsakes either. She didn't have any of my arts and crafts from grade school, no report cards, nothing. Whenever I went to visit friends the first thing I would notice were their pictures. Their walls would be lined with pictures from birth through grade school. Since we were always moving, I would tell my friends, when asked, that my pictures had gotten lost in transition but the reality was there were no pictures. In the fourth grade, we did a project in our Industrial Arts class. The teacher asked us to bring in a baby picture to put in a frame that we had carved out of wood. We were to present the frames to our moms as a present for Mother's Day. I knew I didn't have any pictures, so I repeatedly told the teacher that I forgot to bring it in. After a week of the same excuse, I ended up getting an "E", the lowest grade possible, for the project. I could have just been truthful and said that I didn't have any baby pictures, but I was too embarrassed at the time.

Like I said, when I was young, my mother was mean. She made no attempts at sparing the rod. She was often brutal. Her beatings were relentless, and her words were even worse than the whippings she gave out. I remember the first time she called me a bitch or at least the first time I "remember" being called a bitch. A "little conniving bitch" was what she actually called me. I can remember hearing her say it, but I don't remember what I did that made her so angry. Whatever it was, I don't think any parent should call their daughter a female dog. She was once so angry with me that she choked me until I nearly passed out before she released her grasp from my fragile neck. I can recall so vividly one day deciding that I was going to hang out with my neighborhood friends after school. It was the first time that I would ever go to a go-go. It wasn't late, it was actually after school one day in the school auditorium. The band Trouble Funk was performing. After the go-go ended, my friends and I all walked home together. I lived on Maple Avenue, in Takoma Park, Maryland. It was about a quarter of a mile long and was lined with apartment buildings that ranged from four units to high rises. Because of the close proximity of the buildings, everybody knew everybody. We all went to school together. We played together, and we got into trouble together.

That evening after the go-go at school, as I walked toward my building, which happened to be the first apartment building on the street, I could see my mother walking towards me. Actually, everybody saw her. I could hear the nervous laughter of my friends as someone whispered,

"Oh shit, here comes your Mom."

Before I could think of a way to run without her seeing me, I was being pummeled to the ground. She was quick. The blows were severe. Bruised the most were my ego and self-esteem. I was embarrassed and afraid, and I literally peed on myself. My nose was bleeding, and I took off, running to our apartment. This was not the first or last time that I would be on the receiving end of her brutality or embarrassed in public at the hands of my mother.

It's hard to describe my mother and our relationship. We, my mother and I, the true thespians that we were, could captivate audiences and fool even the sharpest minds into thinking we had the mother/daughter relationship that most envied. It was a farce, the furthest thing from the truth. We tiptoed around our feelings and we weren't open to being expressive without challenging and deflecting our feelings for one another. As the child in the relationship there wasn't much room for me to debate or have any form of rebuttal. She was the adult. She ruled, and most times with an iron fist. As an adult, I still had reservations about expressing my true feelings to my Mom especially as it pertained to how I felt about her and how her abuse of me affected me as a child, teenager and adult. Even now, I know that she wouldn't beat me at this stage of my life, but the fear that she instilled in me as a child by using control and abuse is still there to some degree. I walk a fine line with her.

As a teenager, I acted out and rebelled against her control and abuse. I became a teenage runaway. I ran away over thirty times. I ran away so much that it was nothing for me to leave home for school and not come home for weeks at a time. After a while, my Mother stopped calling the police, and she stopped looking for me. I think she knew that I would turn up eventually because I always did. I always found my way back home. Being a runaway put me in some terrible situations. I would stay anywhere with anybody. I've been stabbed, raped and beaten. I've witnessed murders and came close to being a murder victim myself. Unfortunately for me, none of those things curtailed my habit of running away. The more dangerous the situation, the more toward it I would gravitate. As I saw it at the time, being in the street was better than being at home.

The time I was raped was one of those moments where I was intrigued by danger. I ran away from home one evening. Well, let's just say I didn't go home from school. It was a Friday after school, and I wanted to hang out in DC. We were living in Maryland at the time, and Maryland had a reputation of being too laid back. It was said that only nerds and bammas lived in Maryland. I didn't want to be either, so I had started hanging in DC on the weekends. I left school that day and headed to downtown, DC. It got late and I knew I wanted to go to the go-go that evening, so I didn't go home. Go-Go music was new to the scene in the 1980s but its popularity seemed to grow overnight, and all the teenagers flocked to them on the weekends. Back then you could go to the go-go for five dollars and party until daybreak. The go-go was cool until the crack epidemic took over DC, and things started getting really dangerous. Gun battles were common anywhere there was a go-go. The city was filled with people who either sold crack, smoked cracked, or benefited from someone selling crack. I was a part of the latter. I dated guys that sold crack. If a guy wasn't a drug dealer, I didn't want him. I wanted a bad boy. I was intrigued by the life. The fast life, that brought as much mishap as it did money.

This night, I decided that I was going to the go-go, which was basically a club for teenagers and young adults. I knew that at fifteen-years-old, had I asked permission to go, the idea would have been out of the question in my house, and my mother's answer would have been a resounding "No!" So I decided to just stay out and go anyway. I had befriended an old boyfriend's sister who was much older and became more of an aunt or godmother to me. I knew she would let me stay at her house if I told her my mom said it was okay. She always took my word for truth. I guess she didn't think I would lie to her. Truth was, I told a lot of lies. I also knew that she wouldn't have a problem with my going to the go-go as long as I came back by a specific time. It was getting late and she gave me money to get to the go-go and to get in. She also provided me money to get back to her house when the go-go let out that night. I got there with no problem. I saw people that I knew, but I was there by myself. Rare Essence, the band that was being featured that night, was cranking- that's slang for "they sounded really good." In my day I could dance, and I was in my zone! I loved the attention that I was getting as the guys lined the walls and watched.

Towards the end of the go-go, one of the guys who watched from the sidelines, made his way over to me. He lived around the corner from my godmother. He was also a friend of her brother, my old boyfriend. He asked me how I was getting home, and I told him I was catching the bus. He offered me a ride, which I reluctantly took. I was reluctant for several reasons. One, he was crazy. Two, he was crazy. And three, he was crazy. And yet there I was sitting in the front seat of his car. He was older than I was but not by much. Although I'm not really sure how old he was now that I think about it. I don't remember him being in school at the time. Maybe he had dropped out early. I don't know but I digress. He was a lot more street-savvy than I was, and he was definitely into selling drugs. I had heard rumors that he was a killer, but he didn't look like one, but then again neither did Ted Bundy. What does a killer look like anyway? We had small talk as we cruised through the city listening to music. Much to my surprise, he liked the same music that I did. He was blasting Anita Bakers *The Songstress* album. I was so caught up that I didn't think much about it as he drove passed my godmother's neighborhood. I thought we were just going for a ride. I was enjoying the music and his conversation. He didn't seem as crazy as everybody had made him out to be. He asked if I had ever ridden a motorcycle and I told him no.

He was known for his love of motorcycles. I would occasionally witness him riding them recklessly up and down the streets of his hood.

He began telling me crazy stories about being blamed for murders that he didn't commit and how he wasn't a killer but wouldn't have a problem killing if he had to. I was getting uncomfortable and had enough sense to be a little scared but not enough to ask him to let me out of the car or to take me home. We continued to ride, and I realized that we were no longer in D.C. I would later learn that we were in Suitland, Maryland. I was unfamiliar with this particular part of town, so I asked where we were going. He didn't respond and kept driving. We finally got to an apartment complex, and he drove to the very back of the parking lot. He parked the car and leaned over to open the glove compartment, and that's when I saw the gun. The wheels in my head started churning.

"You've gotten yourself in big trouble now," I'm saying to myself. "How are you going to get out of this?"

He then turns to me and ask,

"Do you want to be my girlfriend?"

I just shrugged my shoulders. I wasn't really sure what to say. I knew he had a girlfriend and my mind was still focused on the gun. He took the gun out of the glove compartment and placed it on his lap.

"Take your shorts down," he said.

I laughed nervously, hoping he was playing.

"He knows me," I thought. "I'm little Amy, "Two-Feet," (that was my nickname).

He knew my godmother and was friends with my old boyfriend. This had to be a joke. I would later learn that he wasn't a jokester and this was no joke. I was slapped and choked until I succumbed to his demands. He had his way with me. I prayed through the entire ordeal that I would not be murdered in that car. When he had finished, he gave me some napkins to clean myself up and told me to put on my shorts. My shorts had been ripped during the tussle as he tried to force them down, so I couldn't zip or button them. I just pulled them up and used my shirt to cover the fact that they couldn't be fastened. I didn't know where I was so I didn't try to get out of the car. Plus he had a gun, and I didn't want to risk getting shot. I was too stupid to do anything. I didn't even cry. I sat there with a busted lip and ripped clothes as we rode back to the city in silence. Once we reached the corner of my godmother's house, he pulled over to let me out of the car. Before I exited, he said,

"This is between us, you gave me the pussy, and I didn't take it."

I got out of the car and ran to the house.

Surprisingly, I wasn't too scared to tell someone who in turn convinced me to tell my mother. My mother took me to the police station, and I told the whole story, but I didn't tell the police what happened because I was afraid of him and or because I thought he would try to do it again. No, I told what happened because I was afraid of her, my mother. Telling the story was what saved me from getting a beating for not coming home from school that day. My mother wanted him arrested and I was to identify him. The day before I was suppose to do so, he shot a man standing right next to me on the side of my godmother's house. That sealed it for me, that's the day that I learned the term, "snitches get stitches and end up in ditches." If my memory serves me correctly, no charges were ever filed. After that, anytime he saw me he would give me money. He always had a gift for me, and I always accepted. I was too scared to say no. He would always ask, "Do you want to be my girlfriend?" and then laugh like crazy as I would take off running. That experience helped me to mature a little more. I grew up over night, became more aware, and I wasn't so trusting. I stopped traveling alone especially at night. I never got in the car with a guy that wasn't my boyfriend by myself again. My mother kept a closer eye on me and became a little more protective after that incident, but it was too little, too late. I was spiraling out of control. Nothing she did or said kept me home.

The experience also made me realize that my mother didn't play when it came to her children. She didn't care who you were or what your reputation was, if you messed with her children she was coming after you. She could beat me black and blue but you, oh you would have hell to pay if you tried it. My mother once told me that she would walk on water for me. And although I've never actually seen her "walk on water," I have been privy to witnessing her beat up a child or two over her children. One day I had gotten into a fight with a group of sisters in our neighborhood in Maryland. They came to my house to fight me. Things didn't go as they had planned. They weren't expecting my mom to be home. Instead of them turning around and going about their business, they proceeded to cuss out my mother. That did it! My mother made my sister and me go out and fight and then she came out and beat up everybody! She then told them to go home and get their momma. I didn't have any more problems with them or any other girls from the neighborhood after that fight. I told you she was a complex woman.

My mother was also old school. Children are to be seen and not heard. I didn't talk back. "Thank you" and "No thank you" were a part of my vocabulary. Ma'am and Sir, Mr. and Mrs. were how adults were addressed. Sass was not acceptable under any circumstances. You did what you were told, and you were not allowed to question why. You just did it. Because of this, I was afraid to express myself or to ask questions. I never asked her why she didn't like me. I never asked about my father's absence. I never questioned why he didn't call or visit like my sister's father. Her father would come all the way from California to visit, and he always sent her gifts and money. I never asked why I couldn't visit my father during the summers like some of my friends did with their fathers who weren't in the home. And I didn't dare question how she could love a man that didn't take care of his own child. I had plenty of questions and many feelings, but I just kept it all bottled up inside, while I acted out on the outside.

Now, what I don't want you to do is feel sorry for me. This story is not a pity party. It's about overcoming obstacles, coming into my womanhood, and finding myself. I don't deserve pity, and I'm not looking for any. And don't get it twisted; I was not the perfect child. I did my share of mischief. I gave my mother a fair share of heartache. I lied a lot, I picked up a bad habit of stealing, I skipped school, I dropped out of high school, you name it, and I did it. I was always acting out even knowing what the penalty of my behavior would be later. As I see it now, I started rebelling for attention. It didn't matter that it was negative, as long as I got the attention of my mother. As I saw it when I acted out, my mother responded. She must've cared. Even if she responded with harsh words and violent outburst, she still responded and remember- she would walk on water for me. She would hit first and talk second. And she could talk too! She would lecture me for hours on end. I started reciting her words in my head; I heard them so much. "If you don't get your shit together you're going to end up dead." And the two phrases that hurt the most, "You are more trouble than you are worth" and "You would be better off dead." Those phrases cut the deepest. So deep, that at forty-eight years old, I'm still healing. I have cuts and bruises that are invisible to the naked eye but they are there. Those words were terrible, but there are still some words and beatings that I can't bring myself to write about because the pain is just that great.

Recently while visiting my mom, she started sharing about her past. We were having a candid conversation about life, and she began to vent with anger her feelings of neglect and abuse at the hands of her mother. She spoke of how irresponsible she felt her parents were as it pertained to how she and her siblings were raised. She talked about being left to fend for herself for days at a time while my grandmother was out living her life as if she had no children. I recognized the hurt and anger. I saw the little girl that wanted nothing more than to be loved by her mother. I had never seen my mother that vulnerable. She was a little girl at that moment, and I wanted to reach out and console her. She was my mother, and I loved her. I hated to see my mother suffering. The things she expressed about her mother were everything I felt about her. It was as if my mother had gotten hold of my journals. How could you feel this way about your mother and as a mother, do the exact same thing to your own children? How could you recognize your mother's failures and shortcomings and not recognize your own? She didn't remember or didn't want to remember the times that I had to take care of my little sister because she was out partying. How she would beat me when she came home from partying to find my sister and I gone. I remember calling a friend and telling her that my sister and I were in our apartment alone and we were hungry. She told her mother, who came to our apartment and got us and left a note for my mother. My mother was pissed. I think she tried to beat me within inches of my life that day. She was mad that I told them we were hungry. She didn't want to appear to be neglectful. She must have read my mind because she stopped long enough during her venting to tell me she was sorry.

"If I've done anything to hurt you, I'm sorry."

I wanted to hug her and tell her that it was okay and that I had forgiven her long ago. I wanted to pray for her and with her at that moment. But I couldn't, and I didn't. It shouldn't have been an "If I hurt you." Why couldn't she just acknowledge that she abused me? Abuse is awful but being abused at the hands of your own mother is incomprehensible. I could never understand it. And although I can't understand it, I made the decision to forgive. I needed to forgive my mother as much as I needed forgiveness. We do better when we know better. As adults, we fail to realize that children don't stay children forever. The things they see, hear and experience aren't lost once they become adults. Perpetrators forget or maybe not, but believe me when I tell you most times the victim does not.

My mother was not a monster. I was not beaten or punished for everything I did or didn't do, and I wasn't hit every day, although at times it appeared so. She had a soft side, the side that did everything she could to be a good mother. When she operated from her soft side, we had good days. On good days, my sister and I were awakened to the smell of pancakes, bacon and eggs (the latter to which I hated). This was usually followed by a ride downtown by car or train to visit the museums. We would enjoy exploring each museum. My mom was the perfect well-informed tour guide. She would explain to us what most of the artifacts were and what each meant to the history of our country. On good weekends we would find ourselves at my uncle and aunt's house enjoying good food and music and playing with our cousins. My mother introduced us to music. She loved Reggae, Jazz and a little Rhythm and Blues. She would take us to Caribbean festivals. But she hated Oldies but Goodies. I think they reminded her too much of her childhood. We listened to music from Norman Brown, James Ingram, Aretha Franklin, Anita Baker, and Luther Van Dross but none of that Motown stuff. She hated the Supremes.

It was important to my mom that my sister and I were well behaved in public. She would take us to restaurants and teach us how to sit like ladies. She taught us how to properly use silverware. We knew the difference between a salad fork and a dinner fork. We knew to put our napkins on our laps and not to talk with food in our mouths. She told us that it wasn't proper to leave our napkins on the table when we finished dinner. The napkins were to be placed on the seat of the chair. We had impromptu picnics and rides to the nearby beaches. She even sent us to church on Sundays. She wouldn't go, but she would dress us up so pretty and send us on our way on Easter. Those were our good days, and they were plentiful. But baby on the bad days, it was bad, and there was always hell for me to pay.

So you see, to me my mom had a split personality. One personality was mommy, the loving, intelligent, fight for her children till the death of you mommy and the second, was Nancy (what I called her behind her back), the mean, quick to anger, no questions asked mommy. This split personality trait is what made me dislike her. I never knew from day to day which mommy I was waking up to, coming home to or going to bed to. I'm the eldest of my mothers' three children. My sister and brother never experienced the kind of brutality at the hands of our Mother that I experienced. My sister did get some spankings and punishments, but they mostly happened because of me. I don't recall my mother actually beating her the way she beat me. My sister may beg to differ but hey, this is my truth and my story. My brother may have gotten a spanking twice. And one of those times he and my cousin almost set my aunts house on fire.

I don't have any explanations as to why they were treated differently when it came to being disciplined except that we all had different fathers. My siblings both had fathers that were a part of their lives. Mine was incognito. My sister's Dad had moved to California for work, but he was very much a part of her life. He visited on occasions. She always received birthday and Christmas presents. My sister would later go to live with her father and his wife in California. She graduated high school out West and came back to DC after her high school graduation. Marrying my brother's dad was the best thing that my mother ever did for me. He and my mom married when I was about seven or eight years old. They eventually split and divorced by the time I was about thirteen but it was enough time for his presence to have a huge impact on me.

The years that my stepdad was in our home were pivotal years for me. We developed a strong father/daughter bond. We became very close. So close, that people actually believed he was my biological father. His presence almost made me forget the fact that I didn't have my own dad. He came to my rescue many times when my mother was upset with me, or at least he tried. She made it clear that there was nothing he could do to protect me because after all, she was my mother. But that didn't stop him from trying. After their divorce, he remained a fixture in my life. He was a true stand up guy. He was my fall guy. He was my knight in shining amour. I thought my mother was jealous of our relationship. Not because he loved me more than her. No, my stepdad loved my mother. He would have done anything to make their marriage work, but I don't think she wanted to make it work and she didn't want him. When it became clear to him that the marriage wouldn't and couldn't work, he decided to sit down and explain to me what was happening. It was such a sad evening. He cried, and I cried. He took off his wedding band and gave it to me as a keepsake. He told me that no matter what happened between him and my mom, he would always be there for me. He was only a phone call away. He told me he loved me, kissed me on my forehead, hugged me and then he left the house, forever. I was devastated, I was crushed and I was furious with my mother. Later that evening, my mother took the ring that he had given me and I never saw it again.

My mom left home, Lynchburg Virginia, when I was just three months old. She told my grandma she was attending a party in DC. She wouldn't return to live there permanently until she was sixty-four years old. She said that she wanted to get away from her controlling mother and overprotective sister. She didn't want to raise her daughter in the same environment that she was raised. She was a country girl that knew nothing about city living. The environment she moved to couldn't have been better than what she had left behind, but she did it her way.

When we first arrived to D.C., we stayed with a friend that she had known from Lynchburg, and we later moved to 14th and Belmont Street, NW in Washington, DC. We lived on the same block as the infamous Pitts Motor Hotel, where Martin Luther King and legendary blues singers like B.B King laid their heads whenever they were in the area. By the time we moved on the street, the Pitts Motor Hotel had become home to the pimps, prostitutes, dope dealers and hustlers of the northwest quadrant of Washington, DC.

I saw a lot on Belmont Street although we only lived there a couple of years. It's where I learned how to run the streets. The apartment building we lived in at the time became a small commune of sorts. Everybody was family. One of my recollections of Belmont Street was an incident that occurred when I was a little more than three or four years old. My Mom and one of her best friends shared an apartment. My mom had gotten into an argument with a gentleman that lived across the hall from us over a stolen television set or stereo. I believe he stole it from our apartment. My mother, never one to back down from an argument, proceeds to cuss the guy out over the stolen object. He hit her, knocking her to the floor. My mother got to her feet, went into our apartment, and retrieved a gun. I don't know why there would be a gun in our apartment except that the area we lived in was pretty shady. The guy ran into his apartment and slammed his door just as my mother began firing shots. Fortunately for him, the four bullets struck the door and not him. The police were called, and my mother was hauled off in handcuffs. It was the first time I "ran away." I walked away from the apartment building and wandered up the street to the park because I didn't think my mommy would be coming back from jail. I can't recall who found me that day or when they discovered that I had gone missing, but I was eventually found. My mother was released that night. The police were unable to find the gun that she and her friend smuggled out of the house by nicely wrapping it inside a blanket along with my baby sister.

Belmont Street was the ghetto. The scenery was like that of an old Shaft movie. I saw a person overdose on heroin and be revived by EMT using some type of smelling apparatus. I witnessed the ice cream truck man being beaten within inches of his life for trying to cheat a child out of some money. I watched in horror as my uncle tried to beat the life out of my sister's father when he found out that he had slapped my mother. I even witnessed a suicide.

Belmont Street was my first experience with the death of a loved one. One of my mothers' closest friends at the time lost her children to a fire in the apartment building where we lived. She and her two children lived in an apartment one floor down from us. One day, the friend left her children in the apartment to visit another apartment in the building. Somehow the children started a fire and were unable to get the door to the apartment opened to escape. By the time the fire department was able to put out the fire, the children were found together, hugging one another under the coffee table. One was pronounced dead at the scene, and the other was taken off the ventilator a couple of day's later, brain dead. It was the first time I saw my mother or any mother grieve over the loss of a child.

Belmont was a street that the cops visited often, and the ambulance operators were often afraid to drive through. Speaking of ambulance operators and death, I almost lost my life on Belmont. One day while following behind an older girl, I attempted to climb the stairs of our apartment building because the elevator was always out of order. At the time, a moving company was delivering a refrigerator to one of the apartments. The men that were moving the refrigerator told us that it was okay to pass them on the steps. The older girl went up before me with no problem. It was my turn next, and as I ascended the steps, one of the movers slipped. He couldn't hold onto the refrigerator, and the next thing I knew it was on top of me smashing my little five-year-old frame into the wall at the bottom of the staircase. By the time they were able to lift the refrigerator off of me, the damage was done. My right ear had been sliced almost completely from my face. I would be scarred for life. So notorious was Belmont Street at that time, the ambulance never came, and my mother had to walk me to the hospital about six blocks away from our apartment building. I had to walk holding my ear to my face for fear that it would fall to the ground. There was blood everywhere- on my clothes, in my hair and dripping down my hand. I had lost so much blood I had to have several blood transfusions. I was hospitalized for a long time. Exactly how long, am not sure, but I do know that out of the many visitors that I had during my stay, my father wasn't one of them. It's funny how we can recall certain things from our childhood but can't remember what we ate on yesterday. He may have called to check on me. Maybe he was doing a stint in jail. I just know he didn't come see me. I was facing a possible death, and he didn't come see about me. We had a lawsuit against the refrigerator company, and I was awarded money for pain and suffering. I was a minor, and my mother was given stewardship over my finances until I turned eighteen at which time I was to receive the money. By the time I turned eighteen, all the talk of the money had ceased. Till this day, I don't know what happened to it; I've always been afraid to ask her.

There were also good times on Belmont. There was always a party, a celebration for every birthday, and holidays were a big deal. House parties were plentiful with all the food, drinks, and music you wanted. There were also plenty of drugs. I didn't realize until I was older, that a lot of the residents in the building were drug users. I saw the needles, and even wondered about the spots of blood that would be on the walls or floors whenever one of them left a bathroom, but I was too young at the time to know what it was all about and I didn't dare ask.

After living on Belmont Street, we moved to the South East quadrant of Washington, D.C. This was where my mother and stepdad met. At the time, my stepdad was living with his sister in the building next door to us. I remember thinking he was so handsome and skinny. Their romance bloomed and things started moving fast. After a short courtship, we moved with him to Takoma Park, Maryland. Takoma Park was such a beautiful place to raise a family, with tree-lined streets, picturesque parks, creeks, great schools and a mixture of races. Takoma Park was where I met my first white friend, Beth Shapiro. Up until this time, I had been in predominantly black neighborhoods and schools. I had never been around white people before Takoma. I met my first best friend, Nicole Marr. It's where I won my first fight and where I lost my first fight to Aretha Lockett. I lost my virginity in Takoma Park. Takoma Park is where I realized that I loved to write and I loved to read. I developed my love for reading at the Takoma Park public library. I read the book *Roots* by Alex Haley in two weeks at nine-years old. Takoma Park is where I smoked my first joint of reefer and took my first drink of alcohol. It's where I learned to swim like a fish. Takoma Park, Maryland is where I experienced the majority of my firsts. Whenever anyone asks me where I grew up, I proudly say, "Takoma Park." Takoma Park was a beautiful place but with all its beauty, it's where I begin to see the ugliness of my mothers' abusive behaviors.

Like I said earlier, I did a lot that warranted punishment but I never thought I deserved to be abused. No child deserves to be abused. Like the time she beat me outside in front of my friends after I came home from the go-go. Imagine being a twelve-year-old little girl, short in statue and skinny, being beaten until you urinate on yourself. Afraid to bathe afterwards because the welts would sting when the water touched them. I've been beaten with switches, belts, rulers, shoes and fist. The worst of the beatings occurred when she used her hands. She would beat me until she tired or until my stepfather intervened. One beating was so bad I began slipping into unconsciousness as she choked me. My little sister ran out of the room to get my stepfather to help pull her off of me. I used to pray that God would send my biological father to rescue me, but that never happened. I remember getting a beating because I snuck to use the phone one night. The beatings became so bad that I had taken to sleeping in the car rather than going home. My mother always kept her car door unlocked so I would just sleep there. One night in the dead of winter, I slept in a neighbor's car. I had come home after dark and tried to get in my mother's car but it was locked. Rather than facing her wrath, I broke into the neighbor's car behind our apartment building and slept there until morning. I don't remember what happened when I went home that morning. Maybe nothing. As I said, I wasn't beaten everyday. There was another time that I had gotten a bad report card, and I just knew that my mother would kill me. She had already called home from work to let me know that "my ass was grass." So instead of waiting in nervous anticipation for her arrival, I left.

I don't remember how I got to my destination, but I somehow managed to get from Takoma Park, Maryland to 17th and Kalorama Road, NW in Washington DC during a snowstorm. My uncle and aunt lived in a house on Kalorama Road, and by the time I got there, it was dark and really snowing. Like a dummy, I forgot to call before I came and as luck would have it when I got there, no one was home. I ended up sleeping on their front porch in the snow until the next-door neighbor happened to see me and brought me into their home. I slept on the neighbors couch that night. When my aunt got home the next morning, she came and got me and called my mom begging her not to punish me. I don't think I got a beating that day. Go figure. Things started going from bad to worse for me. I started skipping school, I was fighting all the time and I continued to runaway. At some point, my mother had reached her wits end and decided to put me in a group home for teenage runaways called "The Open Door." I stayed there for thirty days. I was a model resident. I did everything that was expected and more. I was released after the thirty days and before the week was out, I had run away again.

After Takoma Park, we moved back to DC and by this time I was getting older. The older I got, the fewer beatings I received, which I contributed to the fact that I stayed away from home so much. I always managed to befriend someone who had a large family. It was something that I longed for, a big family. I don't know why I was attracted and intrigued by large families, but I was. It may be because my own family was so small. I was welcomed into two of my girlfriends' homes to live while I was in high school. I never had a problem with finding people that would let me live in their home. I stayed with one friend during the 10th grade and the other while in the 11th grade.

It's not that I couldn't stay home. The rules were

plentiful, but I could have lived there if I wanted to. My mother never said that I couldn't live at home. I actually had a beautiful home to go to. My mother had a nice place that was often nicer than where I was staying. My sister and I shared a room, but it was always nicely decorated. We always had a beautiful place, but we moved around a lot. My mother wasn't really stable. I don't think we ever lived in one place more than two years and that was pushing it. I hated moving. It always meant new schools and new friends. Unlike my sister, I wasn't a social butterfly, and I didn't meet friends easily. Initially, the friends I met were bad for me. It wasn't until ninth grade that I started to choose better friends. And for some odd reason, girls always wanted to fight me. I don't think I had a lot of mouth, but I did say what was on my mind. I tried to stay out of trouble, but no matter where I went, trouble followed me. I would say most times it was jealousy. After all, I was my mother's child. I was nice looking, I had a nice shape and the boys were attracted to me.

To have a sense of stability and to avoid moving and changing schools, I would ask my friends' parents if I could stay with them and go to school from their house. The answer was always yes. Most of my friends' parents loved me. I only wished at the time that I felt that love from my own parents. I'm not saying that my parents didn't love me, but I am saying that I didn't often feel it. My mom tells me she loves me all the time now that I am an adult, almost every time we talk and I know she truly does. If only I could have felt that love as a child, maybe, just maybe I could have avoided some of the many mishaps that I experienced growing up. Perhaps I would have even liked her.

By now you may be thinking, "Why doesn’t she dislike her dad as well?” I guess my answer could be, you can’t miss what you’ve never had. But that’s not true. I did miss him and wanted so badly for him to step up in his role, but he never did. My stepdad did the best he could to fill the void, but it wasn’t enough. I needed someone to call my own. I needed someone to call Daddy. I can’t say that I didn’t like my father because I honestly didn’t know him. I really don’t have too much to say about my biological father’s role in my upbringing except this, “He was absent and I felt his absence every single day of my life.”

CHAPTER TWO
LEAVE AND CLEAVE

"Therefore shall a man leave his father and his mother, and shall cleave unto his wife: and they shall be one flesh."
Genesis 2:24

After the marriage of my mother and stepfather ended, we moved around a lot but DC became my home and my stomping grounds. I love to claim uptown as home and some of my friends are quick to point out jokingly, "girl you know you are a Maryland girl."

I gave my life to Christ at the age of nineteen. The father of one of my high school friends whom I was living with at the time was a trustee at a Baptist church located in downtown, Washington, D.C. and I started attending Sunday services with him. It was something about being in the house of God that made me feel at home. It was like a breath of fresh air and each Sunday I went made me long for the next Sunday. I couldn't wait for the doors of the church to open. I joined the choir and started attending Sunday school.

Although I went through the motions of confessing with my mouth and believing in my heart, controlling my flesh would be a problem for me. It challenged me every day. I went to church and had a form of godliness, but I denied the power thereof. I was still fornicating, and doing pretty much everything that I had done before I started going to church every Sunday until one tragic event changed my life and my walk with Christ.

Like a lot of people's experience with salvation, I was very zealous. I had zeal but no knowledge. I was too "heavenly minded and no earthly good." My boyfriend at the time, my high school sweetheart, did not appreciate my zeal. We started having issues in the relationship because I wanted to practice celibacy and wanted to get married. He wasn't going to let me pressure him into marriage and hadn't yet given his life to Christ. In other words, we were unequally yoked. Since the relationship had started to wane, I started seeing another gentleman who also wasn't saved. He actually had a girlfriend before I met him. I knew his girlfriend and had hung out with her a couple of times before they became an item. She was a friend of one of my good friends. I had no business dating him because, like him, I was also in a relationship. Not only was this new guy not saved, he was also what you would call a thug. He was "street." Salvation didn't curb my fascination of living on the wild side, and so I continued to see this other guy.

We both broke up with our significant others and

became an exclusive couple. At least that's what I thought. It wasn't until his ex-girlfriend literally tried to kill me that I realized I had been played. One day while at a birthday party for my "new" boyfriend's little cousin, the boyfriend's ex-girlfriend ambushed me. I was stabbed and beaten nearly to death. In a fit of rage, this young lady unleashed on me a fury that I have never witnessed and hope to never see again in my life. I prayed to God that she wouldn't kill me as I staggered out of the house and into the backyard to escape. Looking at her face in that moment was like looking into the face of a demon. She was enraged. So much so, that she was foaming out of the mouth. It wasn't long after that prayer that a stranger rushed out his house and rescued me from her wrath. Someone had called 911, and the police and ambulance came, and I was rushed to the hospital. That day I learned and internalized my very first scripture, Psalm 118:17 *"I shall live and not die and declare the works of the Lord."* I was lying in a hospital bed with several stab wounds, a swollen face and a broken heart. And to think I left my boyfriend, someone I knew loved me, to deal with a man that was quite the opposite. I learned a valuable lesson that my mom tried to teach me very early on; "Love the one that loves you." It's true, I was so busy chasing something that wasn't mine and all the time I had someone that was standing there waiting for me to get myself together.

After that day I began to experience God, as I had never done before. I broke off the relationship that almost got me killed, and I started focusing on my relationship with God. He became real and not a figment of my imagination. I got into the Word of God and studied day and night, but it was a struggle. My new life fought against my old life almost daily. It's like when the Apostle Paul says in the book of Romans *"...when I would do good, evil is present with me."* I wanted God and I knew I needed Him but I also knew the streets. And because my life in the streets was familiar, I often found myself drawn to my old life. More times than I care to remember my old life won the battle. Eventually, I threw up my hands and decided for God I live and for God I die. I gave it all up. My old life was behind me, and I was pressing towards the mark. Or so I thought.

I hadn't seen my high school sweetheart for several years; he started dating another young lady shortly after our breakup, and we both were living our lives. He was still in the streets, and I was active in the church. His lifestyle eventually caught up with him, he was arrested and had to do a little stint in jail. We kept in touch regularly through letters and occasional phone calls. We remained good friends, so I always accepted his collect calls. I had a great relationship with his mother and sister, and sometimes they would take me with them when they visited him at the camp where he was sentenced to serve his time. I'm pretty sure he had a girlfriend then, but we were still friends, and I didn't mind being kept abreast of his wellbeing. It may sound weird, but I was kind of glad that he was incarcerated. It meant that he wouldn't meet the fate of death in the streets as so many of the young men in my city did during the crack era of the eighties and nineties. I still loved him and didn't want anything to happen to him. I also thought that I would be able to introduce him to Christ. Every letter that I wrote included scriptures for salvation. I kept him up-to-date on my life with Christ. Whenever I accepted one of his calls, I would fill him in on my experiences at church, and tell him about the different conferences and classes that I attended with the church. He always listened with excitement and appeared to be happy with the changes I had made in my life.

I was back living with my mom. I moved in with her, her boyfriend and my sister (my brother was now living with my stepfather and came over on the weekends). Living with my mother made it easier for me to live righteously. I wasn't as easily tempted as I had been when I was staying with friends. She lived on the outskirts of the inner city, and I didn't have easy access to my old life. I could stay on the right track. I could leave the past behind me.

One day while I was in the house alone, my old boyfriend called from jail. His call came straight through like he was calling from home. He didn't always call me collect, so I didn't think anything of it. We shared small talk, as usual, and I filled him in with what was going on outside of the jail walls. He told me he had to go because they were getting ready to do count and that he would call me later that night. About fifteen minutes later, the buzzer from the front door of the building rang to our apartment. I knew my mom's boyfriend had gone to the grocery store and was coming right back soon. Thinking that it was he I buzzed him in the door. I walked to the apartment door to open it and help him with the groceries and screamed when I saw who was standing there.

It wasn't my mom's boyfriend; it was Bernard, my high school sweetheart, the love of my life, standing in front of me in the flesh. There was no count because he was no longer in jail. There he was standing before me, “looking like a snack.” All my inhibitions went out the window. We ended up having a whirlwind relationship. Things were moving fast and the next thing I knew, we were back as if we had never left. We got an apartment together, and things were okay for a while, but then conviction started setting in. I was right back at square one. In a relationship that I knew wasn't fruitful. I thought, with my zealous self, that he was going to conform to my new life. I just knew he was going to get saved and we were going to get married.

Two things happened: he didn’t get saved and we didn’t get married. As a matter of fact, I ended up putting him out after I realized that once again, I let my flesh get me out of the will of God. He went to live with his sister, and I kept the apartment. I wouldn’t see or hear from him again for about a year. The next time I saw him, he had a girlfriend and a baby.

I was invited by a gentleman friend to attend a weeknight bible class at his church. I had met him at the church when I attended a gospel concert there. It was a Pentecostal church and I loved it. The class was so compelling that I started going every week. My spirit was being fed each week as I attended the class and I soon started going to the Sunday morning services.

Every year the church held a weeklong, New Years revival. The preacher was always Bishop T.D. Jakes. I had been following Bishop Jakes’ ministry for sometime and had even gone to West Virginia to attend his Back to the Bible conferences. My friends and I decided to go to the revival and Wednesday night was my night. Bishop Jakes preached a sermon with the title, *"The Other Son"* (or something similar). His text was from the book of Genesis, and he so eloquently told the story of two brothers, Isaac and Ishmael, blood brothers born under different circumstances. The brothers shared the same father but had different mothers. One son was born out of the need to feed the flesh, and the other was born out of the need to fulfill a promise.

By the time T.D. Jakes had the altar call, I was laid prostrate before the Lord. I felt the power of the Holy Spirit. It was different, and I had never witnessed anything like that before in my life. I gave up my membership of the church I had joined at nineteen years old and joined Greater Mount Calvary Holy Church shortly after that revival. I found myself in my pastor's office asking for his blessing to change churches. It didn't go over well. He was upset at my leaving and didn't or didn't want to understand my reasons for leaving. I was growing. I was hungry and thirsty for the things of God and nothing would deter me from obtaining those things.

My experiences at Greater Mount Calvary Holy church altered and changed the trajectory of my life forever. Bishop Alfred A. Owens and his wife Co-Pastor Susie C. Owens were true powerhouses and soldiers for the true and living God. They preached with conviction and walked in integrity. Co-Pastor preached a sermon about the foolish bridesmaids the day that I joined. I remember it like it was yesterday. Deciding that I would not be likened unto one of the foolish bridesmaids, I rededicated my life and joined the church. Several of my friends from my old church were present for support. It was one of the best decisions that I had ever made.

At Greater Mount Calvary, I learned about the Holy Spirit. I learned the importance of tithing and giving. I gained a wealth of knowledge through the church's Bible educational programs. There were plenty of classes and plenty of services to attend. I had befriended the mother of the gentleman who invited me to Calvary and she became my mentor. She became the Naomi to my Ruth. Here is a little background for those of you who are not familiar with the story of Naomi and Ruth:

Naomi is an Old Testament figure (Israelite) that was credited for saving the life of her daughter-in-law, Ruth. There is an Old Testament book named after Ruth that details their story and it would behoove you to read it during your leisure. The story takes place in the days where judges ruled before Israel would receive their first king, Saul. Naomi was married and with her husband, she had two sons, Mahlon and Chilion. A famine came to their land and the family relocated to Moab. Naomi's husband dies during the famine and she later loses both of her sons. She's left a childless widow with nothing but her two daughter-in-laws. While in Moab during the famine, her sons had wed Moabite women. Grief stricken, home sick and destitute, Naomi decides she wants to return to her home in Bethlehem where she has family. It was not unheard of for a wife of deceased husband to continue to stay and live with the husband's family. Naomi's daughter-in-laws continued to reside with her after the death of their spouses. Before returning to her home, Naomi tried to convince them both to stay in their own homeland with their families but Ruth (one of her daughter-in-laws), decided it best to go with Naomi. She had accepted the life, laws and ways of Naomi's people. She believed in Naomi's God.

Staying with Naomi ended up being the best decision that Ruth could have made as she takes the advice of Naomi and positioned herself in a way that caused her to be noticed by a wealthy landowner whose land she would work. Long story short, Ruth marries Naomi's relative, Boaz, who owned the land that she worked and eventually bore him a son. That son would later become the grandfather of King David and later an ancestor to my Lord and Savior Jesus Christ.

My Naomi always gave me sound advice. She prayed with me and for me through some of my darkest hours. Here advice was not always wanted and sometimes seemed harsh, I always knew it was because of her love for me. She taught me how to maneuver through life as a Christian woman.

There were plenty of opportunities to serve at my church. I joined the youth ministry and became a youth leader and I was even appointed to the Associate Missionary Board by the Bishop. I thought that I had conquered my flesh. The worst of my days were behind me. Little did I know the devil was waiting and strategically planning my fall, and boy would I fall.

After salvation, I thought the next steps would be marriage and kids. My biological clock was ticking. I wanted to be married by the age of thirty, and I was determined to make it happen and I had a plan. Every man I met became a victim of my plan. Unbeknownst to them, they were being put through my little secret test. Were they saved? Did they go to church? Did they have a job? Could they be around me without trying to sleep with me? Oh, and did they have a beard? LOL, I loved a man with hair on his face. I know, trivial right? But hey, I wanted what I wanted. I met many that had most of these attributes, but It didn't take me long to discover that I couldn't look at the outward man. Men were human. In church or out of church, they were more of the same. The difference was God. Saved men repent of their sins, but they are not without them. I dated a man on every point of the spectrum in church. They were babes in Christ, lay members, famous gospel singers, and ministers, and every last one of them failed my test.

I started thinking I was unreasonable with my standards. Maybe I was being too picky. Just because they didn't go to church every Sunday as I, didn't mean they weren't saved or didn't love God, right? WRONG! It wasn't a question of whether they went to church or how much time they spent in church. It was about how they lived outside of the church building. I learned that many of them were in church every time the doors opened, but they weren't the Church when they were outside the building. So I stopped expecting my prince to come from the church. And then it happened- I met a wolf in sheep's clothing. He said all the right things and had a form of godliness. His mother was saved, and they had their own little family church. He would go to church with me (if I asked) and didn't try to sleep with me (initially). He was well into his career and even owned property. And the best thing, he had a beard. He also had two children by two different women, but he was a good father. He had custody of his son and had shared custody of his daughter with her mother. Everybody has a past, so I ignored those little red flags.

In my haste to get married and to marry rather than burn, I married the wrong man. With all of his "good qualities," all of the flags were there from the beginning. He was a habitual liar. He lied about women. He lied about work. He lied about church. He just lied. I should have seen it coming, but I was stuck on stupid. By the time he proposed I was too far in to say no, besides, the diamond was big! There is a scripture Proverbs 14:12 "*There is a way that seems right to a man, but its end is the way of destruction.*" Well that's exactly what happened.

I married him but didn't tell any of my church family, especially my mentor, until after it was over. Why? Because I knew that their discernment would see through what I was trying to hide. I didn't want to be accountable to anyone, and I didn't want anyone to say, "Amy, this is not God." I even went as far as going to Jamaica to do my vows, that way I wouldn't feel bad about not inviting anyone. I was married on April 26^{th,} and on May 30^{th,} I caught him cheating. I did what most people do when they know they've screwed up and am too embarrassed to admit it. I hid my marital problems and I tried to make the marriage work. I used scriptures to justify my foolishness. I fasted, and I prayed, and he still cheated. He was habitual. And I was miserable. There's a story in the Bible where King David was caught in the act of adultery. God told him that the son that was conceived out of this act would die. David fasted and stretched out on the ground, refusing to get up as long as the child was alive. He stayed in that position until he heard his servants whispering that the baby was dead. Once he learned that the baby was dead, he got up, cleaned himself, changed his clothes, and then went into the Lords house to worship. Unlike David, I refused to believe that the baby (the marriage) was dead. I fasted and prayed for a long time, longer than I should have.

I wasn't going to church regularly anymore, I avoided the people that I knew would call me out of my mess and my prayer life was lacking. I left my husband three times and went back each time except for the last. As they say, the third time is a charm. I don't know what made me stay as long as I did, but something in me felt like I could change him and make him want to be faithful to me. I wanted him to be what my father wasn't, and he just didn't have the capacity to be that. He didn't have to. He didn't have to fill my fathers shoes. It wasn't his job to be what my father wasn't. Only God can fill voids. He's a Father to the fatherless. When I came to this realization, I was able to leave without reservation or hesitation.

Recently, I had an "Aha" moment. I was doing some much-needed cleaning of my closet and decided to go through some old tote bins where I kept a lot of my old paperwork and things of the sort. I came across a couple of journals that I had from some years back when I was doing a lot of writing. It was funny to read some of my writings. A lot were actual prayers that I had written out to God in hopes that if I penned my request, they would be taken seriously. Thank God that He is omniscient. Some of the things that I prayed were downright ridiculous. I mean seriously, when you don't know better, you definitely don't do better! I wouldn't say I was a fool in love at the time, I'll just say I was a fool. I prayed for some of the craziest things and people. I certainly believed the scripture "Write the vision and make it plain" Habakkuk 2:2. I did that. I wrote it. I made it plain. I made my request known unto God. BUT God knew best and He made the vision RIGHT!

Loving my current husband, Bernard, the way that I do, and knowing him for as long as I have, it's hard to believe that I could have ever loved another man. The truth of the matter is, according to my journals and written prayers, I've loved quite a few besides him (and I have the prayers written down to prove it...LOL).

I must have been going through a mid-life crisis in my mid-twenties. In just five years, between 25-30 years of age, my journals are a hodgepodge of love, lust and plain stupidity. There was, however, a constant thread- my strong desire to be a wife and a mother. It didn't matter who I was in lust or love with at the time, it was always clear...I wanted to be wife and a mother. I wanted to be a wife and mother so much so that just about every man I met in church, in a church setting or at a church function, was a potential husband and baby daddy.

God has the power to slow time down in order for you to catch up with your own vision. In a five-year time span, I loved, had my heart broken as I watched the love of my life start a family with someone other than me, witnessed someone I thought would be my husband marry someone else, loved again, got married and became a stepmother, realized I wasn't in love, experienced infidelity, got divorced, was given another chance at love, and married again. This time was for keeps! What I realized reading these journals was that God didn't change

His mind. The blue print is the blue print, and it doesn't change. The vision was still being honored. The execution may have changed, and the timeline may have been extended, but the blue print and vision were consistent.

I came across an entry that was written on the first Sunday of August 2009. It was a prayer, and in it I said that within a year to that date, I saw myself with twins. As I was reading the journal, my heart started racing, and tears begin to fall because I knew that God had been listening. He heard and read every word that I had ever uttered or written. He knew what was best for me, and even in my most vulnerable and weakest state of mind, He loved me enough to RIGHT my vision.

More than anything I wanted to have children and to raise them in a healthy home with both mother and father, unlike how I was raised. I desired to have a husband who loved me as much or more than he loved himself like Christ loved the church. I wanted and needed a husband that could handle all of my craziness. One that could handle me when I was frail, who was strong enough to hold me yet tender enough not to break me. All of my previous relationships had paled in comparison to the friendship/relationship that I have and have always had with my husband. God allowed me to go through the heartbreaks and headaches so that I could appreciate the king that He was preparing for me. I had gotten it wrong many times. I was searching and finding the wrong man. My husband found me. I was his choice in high school. But I was a broken little girl with daddy issues. I went from one bad relationship to another, searching for a daddy. The worse they were and the longer their rap sheet, the more I wanted them. I wanted a man like my father, but God knew better. He knew what I needed. God's word is never wrong, and it never fails, "He who finds a wife finds a good thing" Proverbs 18:2. Thank God none of my prior relationships worked and thank God no children were ever conceived not even in my first failed marriage!

They say love can be better the second time around, and I agree, but it doesn't have to be that way. Jesus only had to die once to demonstrate God's amazing love towards mankind. I believe that we can all get it right the first time if only we would follow and obey God's word. We get off track when we do it our way but God in His infinite wisdom, grace and mercy gives us another chance. He did that for me. He allowed me to experience love in a marriage with a man that loved and honored me.

My high school sweetheart and I found our way to one another, and we got it right. This year will be fourteen years for us and I couldn't be happier. The marriage has not been without difficulty, but what marriage isn't? We've had some weary days but our good days outweighed them. We are the proud parents of three children. My husband had a son during a previous relationship and by God's grace we have twins, a boy and a girl. I told you, God saw the vision. We write the visions and God RIGHTS the visions. Write your visions!

CHAPTER THREE
MIRACLES

"And these signs shall follow them that believe."
Mark 16:17

I assumed it only natural that my husband and I would immediately start a family, but nothing for me has ever been immediate or easy. My husband already had a child. Things didn't turn out the way he imagined. He was convinced that having another child would produce the same results or maybe even worse. Don't get me wrong, he loves his son but the drama and trauma that came with being an unwed father, left a less than appetizing taste in his mouth about fatherhood. But that's his story, so let's get back to mine. We, well actually I, decided it was time to start a family. I didn't have to try hard to convince him that our love was strong and consistent. Having a family was worth giving a try. Our marriage was intact and nothing but good could come out of us having a child of our own.

We began to work on getting pregnant. After being married for three years, guess what? Nothing happened. Three years, absolutely nothing. No false positives, no miscarriages, no missed menstrual cycles, nothing. I was thirty-five and had never been pregnant. I was crushed. What could've been wrong? I was married. I wasn't fornicating. There was no infidelity. I was living for God, going to church regularly, and paying my tithes and giving offering. I was doing my best to live holy and nothing was happening. As far as I knew, I didn't having any ailments that would prevent me from getting pregnant.

It appeared that no one else I knew was having this issue. Pregnant women surrounded me. My co-workers, supervisors, friends, family members, the teenage-girl next door, married women, single women, I mean everybody was getting pregnant except for me. I felt like such a failure. Was my past coming back to haunt me? Was God punishing me for all of those years I threw caution to the wind? No, that's not God. Or was it? There had to be something wrong with me. Every woman should be able to have a child. Women were created to be a helpmeet and to procreate. I was depressed. I was trying to mask it. I was smiling on the outside and crying on the inside. We decided it was time to seek help after the third year of trying. That year on New Years Eve of 2009, a friend had prophesied to me that I would get pregnant before the year ended. On Mother's Day, that same friend called and prophesied she would be calling to wish me a happy Mother's Day the next year, 2010.

I found the best reproductive endocrinologist in the area and made an appointment. We had loads of test done.

My husband was fine, he had a high sperm count, and was otherwise healthy. I, on the other hand, was not. It turned out that a pituitary tumor that I had developed several years ago was throwing my hormones out of whack. The tumor, which was located at the base of my brain, left me with elevated prolactin levels. The high levels of prolactin caused my body to produced breast milk. Since I wasn't pregnant the elevation was causing the brain to send the wrong messages to certain parts of my body. The tumor was small and benign, but it was close to the brain. Surgery would not be without risk. The next option was medication. I was started on a Parlodel therapy to lower my prolactin level and increase my chances of conception. The Parlodel worked to lower my levels and even shrunk the tumor, but I still didn't get pregnant. It was then determined that I had unexplained infertility. In a nutshell, they didn't know why I wasn't getting pregnant.

Clomid therapy was the next step in our pregnancy journey. Clomid was a medication that would assist in helping me with ovulation. After the second round of clomid therapy didn't work, Dr. Abassi, my endocrinologist, decided we needed to get aggressive. We did Intrauterine Insemination (IUI), twice, and still, nothing happened. I had two friends who were also trying and having trouble conceiving. Within months of trying, each one called me with the wonderful news that they were pregnant. It was hard not to cry. I was happy for them but Lord, "What about me?" The next step was In Vitro Fertilization (IVF). This was the most aggressive step. If that didn't work, they suggested adoption. The IVF process was scary. It involved my having to inject myself in the stomach daily, having blood drawn every other day, egg retrievals and embryo transplants. We went through the lengthy process and procedures and wouldn't you know it...nothing happened. My pregnancy test came back negative. It was an emotional blow. I did a lot of crying, praying, fasting, and more crying. I was a mess. I woke up every morning at 5 o'clock a.m. to pray and do devotions. I read the same scripture every morning, Romans 4:18-21 *"Against all hope, Abraham in hope believed and so became the father of many nations, just as it had been said to him, "So shall your offspring be." Without weakening in his faith, he faced the fact that his body was as good as dead—since he was about a hundred years old—and that Sarah's womb was also dead. Yet he did not waver through unbelief regarding the promise of God, but was strengthened in his faith and gave glory to God, being fully persuaded that God had power to do what he had promised."* It seemed as if no matter how much I prayed, or fasted, or cried motherhood eluded me.

Thank God for my employer and an excellent insurance plan at the time. After the first IVF procedure failed, we learned that the insurance company allowed for one more IVF round. Not sure what to do, I did what I always did, I prayed. As I drove home from one of my many consultations with Dr. Abassi, torn about what to do next, I asked God. I really wanted a baby but maybe being a mother wasn't in the plan for me. I wasn't up for being disappointed again. The entire process was mentally wearing on me, and I desperately needed guidance for next steps. Sitting at a red light, I looked over to my right and I kid you not, God spoke to me right at that moment. There on the corner at the red light on Old Georgetown Road in Bethesda, Maryland was my answer. I had driven this route for almost a year straight and never saw it. Right there on the corner, was a small consignment shop. The name? *Consider It Done*. For those of you reading this, you have to find God in everything. Look for the signs, listen out for His voice, and know His touch. At this particular point in my life, I looked and listened for God in everything. The scripture came to me in that moment, *"My sheep know my voice and a stranger they will not follow."* I knew at that moment that it was God. We started the next round of IVF and after what seemed like forever, the test results came back positive! The blessings of the Lord are yea and amen. Yes, after years of trying to conceive, just two months shy of my 39th birthday, I was pregnant and guess what? We were having twins! My mother was the second person I told. My due date was May 28, 2010. The great news of being pregnant was coupled with the worst case of morning sickness ever. I didn't just have morning sickness. I had all day sickness that lasted for the first four months of my pregnancy. Other than being sick all day, all was well. I couldn't wait to meet my babies. I was finally going to be a mother.

My pregnancy was high risk. I had to have blood work done every week. Each week my blood levels were as expected, and my sonograms looked great, and showed each baby progressing. The babies were moving and growing. I started to feel the flutters of their tiny kicks. It was Christmas time, and as I did ever year, I took leave from work and wasn't scheduled to return to work until after the New Year. I was scheduled to return to work the first week of January. I was entering my second trimester of pregnancy. I was scheduled to return to work the same day I had my second-trimester workup, which involved my cervix being measured and the babies being measured. It was also the day that I was to find out the sex of the babies. Since I had to report to work that day, I scheduled my appointment for the first thing in the morning. I never made it to work that day. It was the day my entire world would come crashing down around me. The technician doing the sonogram excused herself after scanning my belly for what literally only seemed like ten seconds. The door opened and in walks my ob-gyn. The news was not what I expected and definitely not what I wanted to hear. I was asked to get dressed and meet my doctor in his office. At this time, I tried to will myself not to panic. No longer aware of my surroundings, I was having an out of body experience. I could see myself sitting in front of his desk, and I could see his mouth moving, and I wish I could recall verbatim what the doctor said, but I can't. I don't remember anything except that I was at that moment having a second-trimester miscarriage. My cervix was incompetent, my membranes were rupturing, and an ambulance had been called to take me to the hospital. In a state of shock, disbelief, and disappointment, I didn't wait for the ambulance. Instead, I put on my coat, left out the door, got in my car, called my husband, told him what was happening and what hospital I was going to, and I drove myself to Holy Cross Hospital located in Silver Spring, Maryland. I bypassed admission and went straight to the perinatal ward. I was admitted bedside and began my fifty-day journey to motherhood.

I was admitted and put on strict bed rest. Let me tell you when they said "strict" that was exactly what they meant. I had to lie in the bed in what is called the "Trendelenburg" position, that's where you are flat on your back and the bed is tilted until the feet are higher than the head. I was upside down. I wasn't allowed to get out of the bed, so I had to use a bedpan when I needed to relieve myself. I had to eat lying on my side. I wasn't able to bathe myself and had to wait for my husband or another family member before I got a bath. The worst times for me were when I had to be bathed by a nurse. It was awful. Because of my lying position, my blood pressure dropped which caused by bowels to lock. My third day in the hospital, I was examined by the perinatologist, who bless his heart, tried to be as optimistic as possible and told me about the possibility of using a cerclage to close the cervix. Upon examination, that possibility went out the window. My cervix had disappeared, and I was fully dilated at only nineteen weeks pregnant. My babies weren't even considered babies yet. The babies wouldn't be viable for another several weeks, and here I was ready for delivery. Bed rest was my only hope, that and prayer. Prayer is a posture of thanksgiving, reverence, and submission to God. When you pray, you make your request known to Him. The latter definition seemed more of what was needed at the time, but I had to be thankful for the mere fact that I was even pregnant. There was a time I thought that I would never be a mom. I mean, let's be honest, time as we know it, was not on my side. But I was pregnant, and I knew that I had to give thanks regardless of the circumstances.

I tried to exercise my faith daily because faith without works is dead, but really, if the truth were told, I was scared, and I really did not know what the outcome of this situation would be. I did know that God was able, and even if I miscarried it didn't negate the fact that HE WAS ABLE. Every Thursday marked another week pregnant. So the goal every week was to make it to Thursday. I made it to 20 weeks and that Friday I had another sonogram. Saturday morning in comes Dr. Bad News (that's what we will call my doctor from here on out), with his observation and the results from the sonogram. After he had spoken with the perinatologist and looked over the sonogram, it didn't look good. The cervix was gone, and I was eighty percent effaced. They weren't going to send me home because they were afraid I would bleed out during the miscarriage. I was to stay in the hospital and wait for the inevitable to happen. I was going to lose my babies. I don't know if he thought what he said next would offer some comfort, but it didn't. He told me that women in my position experience this everyday. Second-trimester miscarriages were common. The pregnancy was high risk because of my age and the IVF. We could always try again. We could always try for another baby. Another baby? I didn't want another baby. I wanted my babies, the babies that I was carrying. These babies were the results of my fasting and praying. They were the promises of God. They were conceived out of a Hannah prayer. How could I lose my babies?

My Mother, sister, and nephew were in the room at the time, and upon hearing his prognosis, I started to cry. My Mother, with her very strong personality, couldn't stand to be quiet any longer. She asked the doctor to step in the hallway. She wanted to have some words with him about his bedside manners, or lack thereof. I knew my Mother, so I quickly intervened because it was going to get ugly in the hallway if you know what I mean. I knew her tongue was sharp, and once she started, I didn't doubt there would be a fight. Worst yet, I didn't want them to put me out of the hospital, so I asked my mother to step out of the room so that I could speak with the doctor alone. She stepped out of the room. I asked "Dr. Bad News" to avoid discussing any medical news either good or bad whenever anyone other than my husband was present in my room.

I was a wreck. I never, I mean never, cried so hard and so much in my entire life. My poor nephew was so traumatized that day that he never came back to the hospital to see me, and I was hospitalized for another forty-five days. My sister was the one to help calm me down and bring me back to some sanity. She rubbed my back, wiped my tears and told me to pray.

"You're a prayer warrior," she said.

"Call your friends that know how to pray."

And I did. I called the prayer warriors, and prayers literally went up all over the country. I made it to two more Thursdays. It was a Wednesday before I was to turn twenty-three weeks. I was one week shy of viability. Dr. Bad News was very surprised and couldn't believe that I was still in that hospital bed, in that position carrying those babies. Dr. Bad News and every doctor and nurse in that ward were getting ready to get a lesson in GOD 101. During my stay in the hospital, I was so blessed. My husband came everyday from work and stayed most nights and went to work from the hospital. On the nights that he went home to shower and sleep in a comfortable bed, my mom or mother-in-law spent the night.

My mother was really showing up for me. She would come and stay until the last train left the metro station. I even had a girlfriend spend the night with me one night. I had visitors every day. My brother and sister had become fixtures in my room. My job sent gift packages, fruit, and well wishes. And the people of God were praying. I was still in the hospital and lying in the Tredenlenburg position with locked bowels. I tried my hardest not to push. I was given the orders, no straining, no pushing and no sitting up in bed. My membranes, the water bags, were already leaking and one baby had started to travel down in my vaginal canal.

The body has a way of relieving itself and on that fateful Wednesday evening as my husband slept on the couch across the room, my water broke. Without my pushing my reflexes took over, and my body pushed on it's own. It wasn't trying to get the baby out; it was trying to move the bowels that had been locked for many weeks. I heard a loud pop and felt the water run down my legs. This was what I had prayed wouldn't happen. I screamed, causing my husband to jump out of his sleep. My screams got the attention of the nurses, and before I knew it, there was a sudden flurry of activity and a sense of urgency.

The nurses were running in and out of my room. I was crying and begging God to save my unborn babies and Bernard was trying to be my calm. He never showed it and never said it, but I know he was scared. It was determined that the only thing to do was to wait for the labor, but the contractions never came. The doctor was called, and I was rushed to get a sonogram. We learned that Baby A was in the birth canal, trying to make an appearance despite my not experiencing any labor. The decision was made to keep Baby A in the birth canal, as a stoppage to protect Baby B. Baby A was not expected to make it. They told me to prepare for a stillborn birth. With any luck, they hoped to save Baby B. I wasn't expecting the death of either baby. I could only expect God to work a miracle. I had to believe God. A neonatologist was sent in to advise us of what we had to look forward to should I deliver either baby alive at such an early gestation period. The chances of survival at that time were only 17%. He assured me he would do everything he could to keep them alive if possible, and if that was what we wanted. Everything else would be in the hands of God. Once again, I called on the prayers of the righteous. And yes, prayer does work. The next day came and went...no baby. I was twenty-three weeks pregnant.

Friday came and went...no baby. Saturday came and went...no baby. Sunday, January 31, 2010, while getting bathed by my husband, he says, "Amy, there is something that looks like a hand or foot hanging out of you!" He runs out of the room and calls for the help of a nurse. Again, there was a flurry of activity. Be-Be, the nurse assigned to me for the day, jumps on my bed and grabs and opens a pair of sterile gloves. What she does next saved my babies life. She stuck one gloved hand inside of me and pushed Baby A back in and up my vaginal cavity. Her other hand was holding my hand. I was wheeled to labor and delivery, with a nurse at the foot of my bed, with her gloved hand in my vaginal cavity as my husband ran behind. I was thinking to myself "Only I would bring babies into the world in such dramatic fashion."

My doctor was not on call that day, and his partner was not at the hospital either. I have no idea who the woman was that delivered my child, but I do thank God for her. She looked to be a young African American woman, possibly in her late twenties, early thirties. No one was sure how to proceed, and I heard the suggestion being thrown around to do a cesarean. I knew that Baby B was still in its sac and so I strongly objected. I didn't want to risk losing both babies. The young black female doctor told me they wouldn't do a cesarean, but I was going to have to push out Baby A and pray that Baby B stayed put during the process. I didn't understand how I was going to do it. I had never delivered a baby before, but I did exactly that.

I prayed, pushed three times and out came Baby A. I didn't hear a sound. No crying and no whimpering. I looked at the clock, and it was 1:14 p.m. There were no breaths taken. The baby was immediately whisked from my sight and intubated. The next couple of seconds felt like hours. The neonatologist, Dr. Picard appeared. He held my hand and told me that my baby girl was alive. Just like that, I was a mother. I had given birth to a baby girl. And she was alive. By the time my husband was able to clean up and get the scrubs on she was born. They did let us see her before she was rushed to the NICU. I didn't see much because she was so tiny. We named her Logan Nichelle Langley; she was 454 grams, exactly one pound.

I was cleaned up a little and had another sonogram to see if Baby B was in any type of distress. Baby B was okay and still in the same position. I was taken to recovery, and because of H1NI (a viral epidemic at the time), only two people were allowed in recovery to see me. My husband and mother were there and my Mother-In-Law snuck in later. I was examined, and some of my cervix had started to reappear. The Perinatologist was confident that he could perform an emergency cerclage procedure that would hold the cervix closed and hold Baby B in as long as possible. The longer the baby stayed put, the greater the chances of survival. The procedure was successful, and I was sent back to a room in the perinatal ward. I was still pregnant. It was the first time I had ever heard of someone giving birth to twins separately.

Bernard and my mother were allowed to see Logan after a while. I couldn't see her because I was back on strict bed rest. They reported back saying she was so beautiful and looked just like her daddy. I couldn't wait to see the pictures they were allowed to take. When I did, I was shocked. Not only shocked but stunned, surprised, scared, mad, depressed and happy all at one time. No matter what people tell you, you can never be prepared to see your baby so sick. She was so tiny, and there were tubes and IV's everywhere. Her skin was translucent. If you looked hard enough, you could see some of her organs. Her face was flat. It was smashed in from being trapped in my vaginal cavity for so many days. Her hands and feet were small, but her fingers looked long, like an alien's. She did not look human. Oh my, is this what my baby looks like? God, what is her life going to be like? How can she recover from this traumatic experience? How can I recover?

Those feelings were replaced by what I assumed only a Mother could feel. It was the most overwhelming and powerful feeling of love. This was my child, my daughter. I birthed her, and she was here and best of all, she was alive. I knew from that day that I would love this baby and the one that I was carrying unconditionally with no strings attached. And whatever it took, they were going to be all right. I was going to be different from my mother and father. There would be no verbal or physical abuse, and I would do my best to always be present. I would not allow my experiences as a child show up in their lives. I would be present for whatever they needed me to be. I also prayed that my husband and I would at all cost, raise them in a loving, respectful, and God-fearing home.

Logan Nichelle Langley was born on January 31, 2010 at just twenty-three weeks and three days gestation. The doctors originally told me that she needed to be 24 weeks for viability. After her birth, they said nothing about viability, they only marveled at the miracle. Her organs were not fully formed. She had a wide range of illnesses from apnea of prematurity, chronic lung disease, retina of prematurity, jaundice, and a PDA (Patent ductus arteriosus), a heart problem. She had to have many blood transfusions. She even developed sepsis. One day she totally bottomed out, just stopped breathing, heart stopped and everything. I happened to be bringing my stepdad and his wife into the NICU at the time, and upon seeing the doctors working to save her life, I almost bottomed out myself. Seeing them work so feverishly to revive my child was heartbreaking. I couldn't take it but I didn't let it show. I kept a brave face. At the request of the doctors, I was rushed out of the NICU and wheeled back to my room. My stepdad and stepmother helped get me back into my bed.

I wouldn't see Logan for another three days. I was too scared to go back. I didn't want to see her in pain. I thought if I didn't go back maybe she would get better. Bernard would go over and report back to me her progress, but I just didn't have the guts to see her. Two of the NICU nurses came over one day and brought some pictures, and one of her diapers. I guess they noticed that I hadn't been over to see her. Her diaper was so small I had mistaken it for a panty liner. Finally, I got up the nerve to go over to the NICU to see Logan, and I'm glad I did, because I met the best NICU nurse on staff. Nina, the nurse on duty at the time, seemed to have read my mind as I wheeled myself around the corner. She made me feel so comfortable as she walked me through all that was going on with Logan without overwhelming me with too much information. She spoke to me in a language that a mother could understand. She spoke in laymen terms, not medical terms or jargon. From that day forward, I went to see Logan everyday until the day I birthed Baby B.

The NICU experience was very daunting. The sounds of the alarms going off were recurrent. And for a parent, every alarm is alarming. You hate it when the nurses take their time coming to see what's wrong because you don't know at the time, that every alarm is not "bad." I got daily updates from the NICU doctors on Logan's progress. Some days were better than others, but most days were terrible. I tried hard not to stress because I was still carrying another child and didn't want to go into labor. I was trying to hold this child in for as long as I could. And I did, for three more weeks. Thankfully my room was directly across the hall from the NICU unit. I was still on bed rest. I couldn't get up to walk, but I could get in the wheel chair and roll across the hall to see Logan for about twenty minutes a day.

Logan was a fighter from the beginning just like me, and she looked just like her Father. She had his features, cleft in chin and all, but she was definitely the daughter of Amy Nichelle, a fighter every step of the way. She overcame odds that were stacked so high against her. She defied the odds. God will use the foolish things of this world to confound the wise.

During this time, we had one of the biggest snowstorms the DMV area had seen in years. It snowed so much that the doctors and nurses on duty were ordered to spend the night for fear that they wouldn't be able to make their next shift if they left. The Metro transit system had shut down, and the power at the hospital went out. The hospital was operating on generators, and I was praying that Baby B would not make an appearance. The trucks that delivered the food were a no show, so I was stuck eating stale sandwiches. I couldn't watch television, didn't have visitors and worst, my husband couldn't even get through the snow. After the first night by myself, I begged Bernard to find a way to that hospital and he did. A twenty-minute ride turned into three hours but he made it. It was now one day before it would be three weeks since Logan had been born and miraculously baby B showed no signs of wanting to come. My belly was getting huge, and I could feel every kick and move. My mother stayed with me that Saturday night to give Bernard a break.

My morning sickness had come back with a vengeance, and I started feeling bad. I told my mother that I felt like the baby was ready to come and she got mad because she thought I was being negative. That night I asked the nurse on duty if she could remove my IV because my arm was getting irritated, and since I hadn't delivered the baby all of this time, I didn't need it. That was a wrong move. The next morning Bernard and my mother-in-law came, and my mom left. I was feeling nauseous and started to feel slightly uncomfortable. I had never been in labor before, and I didn't know what it felt like so I didn't say anything at first. The pain was getting worse, so I finally said something to my husband and nurse about being in labor. The nurse told me I wasn't in labor because she didn't see anything showing on the monitor.

Throughout the morning the pain got worse. As the afternoon approached, the pain came faster, so I said something to the nurse, who again assured me that I was not in labor. Finally, I asked her to call my doctor. Dr. Bad News was not on call, but one of his partners was there to make rounds. The doctor came and looked at the monitor and agreed with the nurse that I was not in labor. Before she could walk out the door, my water broke. My temperature was elevated. I had developed an infection throughout the night after the IV was removed. I was moved out of my room to labor and delivery. This time minus the drama we had with Logan. My mother-in-law and husband were with me, and my contractions increase. It's a lie that a toothache hurts worse than labor pains. Those pains were kicking my butt. I wanted to deliver this baby quickly just like I did with the first. It wasn't happening. With Logan, I was fully dilated and totally effaced at 20 weeks. With this baby, I couldn't dilate pass four centimeters, and my fever was increasing.

I was given a Pitocin drip to help speed up the contractions. It was supposed to help me to dilate. But it didn't. The contractions came quicker and harder, but I still wasn't dilating past the four centimeters. Baby B started stressing with fluctuating heart rates. The heart rate dropped so low at one time, it wasn't even on the monitor. They began to prep me for an emergency cesarean. I'm a trooper and have a high tolerance for pain, but I don't ever want to have to go through that pain again.

The entire procedure took about an hour from prep to delivery, but it felt like forever. The room was cold and sterile. I couldn't see over the blue curtain they had covering me from the neck down. Bernard was holding my hand because they had me strapped down so I wouldn't move. I could feel them tugging and pulling, and oh boy, it started working my nerves! I told the anesthesiologist that I thought I was losing my mind and my life; he assured me that I wasn't. Not long after, I saw the most amazing thing that I had ever seen in my life. My son was born. I had a baby boy born February 21, 2010 at 3:15 p.m. weighing 1lb and 14 oz. He looked like royalty, and we named him David Joshua James Langley. In three weeks, I had delivered two babies, one vaginally and another via cesarean. My struggle with infertility was over. I was a mom, again.

David was breathing on his own and did not require a ventilator, but he was put on the next breathing apparatus down, which is called a CPAP (it looked like a football helmet) to help him out a little. He was taken to the NICU.

Hours later, he had to be intubated. The CPAP wasn't working. I didn't see either baby again for three days because I was in so much pain from the cesarean. I couldn't bear to even sit in the wheelchair.

After the third day, I was released from what had become my home away from home for fifty days. I went to the NICU and held my babies for the first time. I don't think I took a breath the entire time they were in my arms. It was a remarkable feeling. Nina was on duty and was their nurse at the time, and she showed me how to "kangaroo" with them. Kangaroo, holding a newborn "skin-to-skin" is proven through research to help preemies survive the NICU. I could only hold them each for about ten minutes, but it was the most rewarding ten minutes I've ever spent with them.

David like his sister was born with a host of illnesses, chronic lung disease, ROP (Retinopathy of prematurity), PDA, ASD (Atrial septic defect), jaundice and had contracted CMV, a potentially dangerous virus I had never heard of before until then. He would stop breathing and had to be resuscitated more times than I care to remember. One day I walked in the NICU to visit, and my son was literally in a plastic bubble with steam pouring in because his lungs were not cooperating. He was in that apparatus for about two weeks. He received daily nebulizer treatments. He had to have Gancyclovir therapy, which was sometimes given to cancer patients, for six weeks because the CMV had gone to his left eye. Thankfully the Gancyclovir cleared it up, and no surgery was required. He had always been an excellent eater, so he started putting on weight right away, unlike his sister who still doesn't eat much to this day.

During Logan and David's one hundred plus days in the NICU, Logan was the longest NICU resident at the time, all the nurses fell in love with them- especially Nina and Tina. I always felt at ease when Nina and Tina were on duty. Logan had heart surgery to close up her PDA. She also had to have laser surgery on her right eye to repair her ROP. Both surgeries were a success. She was breathing on her own before she left the hospital, and it looked like she would go home before her brother because his heart and lungs weren't cooperating. I didn't want to leave either of my babies there alone so I prayed that they would come home together. I stayed at the hospital everyday. I went back to work, but because I worked so close to the hospital, I would go in before I went to work, on my lunch break and after work. People told me that I needed to get rest but who can rest with their children in the hospital. I was able to feed and bathe my babies because I was there everyday with them, and the nurses and doctors had explained early on that my participation would be instrumental in their healing.

Bernard came to the hospital a lot but not everyday. He did what he could, but as a mother, I had to be there everyday. One day, about three days after I came home from the hospital after having David, I cried all day because I couldn't drive to the hospital. I could barely walk let alone drive. I was a mess, but each day got better, and the more time I spent with them the better the outlook.

Before being discharged from the hospital, they had to pass their hearing test. Logan passed hers but David didn't. The next day someone different came to administered the hearing test. She asked me if I would mind if she held him. I told her I didn't mind. I could tell that there was something special about her spirit. Now I don't know if she prayed while she held my son, but I know I did and in the midst of my praying, I heard the nurse yell, "He passed!" This had been one heck of a ride.

The next day, Dr. Picard, the neonatologist, told me to prepare for my babies to come home. They, yes they, would be going home the following Monday, June 14th together! God is so good! Our NICU journey was over! They were going home! Their NICU stay was one to remember. David had everything Logan had times ten. He was sick, possibly the sickest baby in the NICU during their stay. He coded more times than I care to remember. Unlike his sister, he was never able to have his heart or eyes repaired through surgery because his blood gases were always off level. He had chronic lung disease and a touch of sepsis. He would code several times and had to be bagged in order to bring his oxygen levels back to normal. The most heartbreaking thing I'd ever witnessed was watching my children code and realizing that there was nothing I could physically do to help them. I cried every day the first year of their lives. I probably cried every other day until about their fifth birthday.

One month was particularly bad. The twins were now home, and we were settled into our routine. They both had heart monitors and required oxygen. I was administrating medicine around the clock just as the nurses did in the NICU. Their second birthdays were approaching. We had so many doctors visit and emergency room visits that I felt like I was going to have a nervous breakdown. I was barely holding on to my sanity. Logan was hospitalized for neutropenia and David had been hospitalized for pneumonia.

My husband and I couldn't have a date night because I was too scared to let anyone babysit. I didn't trust anybody to care for them. I had not been to see a movie in over two years. I thought I had gotten more than I bargained for and I couldn't see the light at the end of the tunnel. The old pessimistic Amy began to surface. I was becoming an angry, resentful mother, I found myself depressed, and I was taking it out on my husband. To anybody that would listen, I would say to think really long and hard about becoming a parent. I was complaining everyday about the life God had blessed me with. I was angry that I didn't have help. The help I had initially was dwindling, as the twins got older. Family still came by, but Bernard and I had to do the nightshift on our own. I was resenting the fact that at forty-one years old I had children who were so young. I was cursing more than I was praising. To be honest I wasn't even praying consistently. Everything was coming to a head.

Logan had trouble in the NICU eating, and it continued once we were discharged. I wasn't getting any sleep. I was struggling to get Logan to eat. I was trying to get them to a point where they were a little independent and not want me to walk around holding them all the time. One day it all came to a head. They both ended up getting sick. It wasn't bad where I had to take anyone to the emergency room, but they were sick. They had runny noses, were coughing, and whining. They didn't want anyone else to hold them except for me. I couldn't put them in their room when they fell asleep, because they would wake up screaming immediately after I laid them down. Not that they slept in their room all night anyway, but I was able to get a couple of hours. I had to hold each one and rock them to sleep at the same time. One was on my left shoulder and the other was on my right. I screamed so loud that I think I burst my own eardrums. I screamed and they screamed. I realized in that moment, I was suffering from postpartum depression.

A couple weeks after my emotional breakdown, we were invited to a football party and my mother-in-law was gracious enough to watch the twins. I was excited because I would get a chance to be around adults, and not have to hear any crying, whining, or fussing for a couple of hours. We're getting dressed, and I was flat ironing my hair, when David comes in the bathroom. I looked in the mirror to check out my hair, and when I go to reach for the flat iron it was not there. David had them in his hands, one hot plate on each hand. The look of horror on his face was almost too much for me. I wanted to faint but I willed myself not to. He screamed and I screamed all while the flat irons were still in his hands.

I snapped out of my hysteria because I heard my husband running down the steps (he thought David had fallen down the steps because he had taken a liking to the stairs). By the time I was able to get the flat irons out of David's hands, the damage was done. They immediately started blistering. He had second-degree burns on both, blisters on his thumbs, and the tips of his tiny fingers. It was heart wrenching! And there went my night out.

Instead, I spent the night in the emergency room, praying that CPS didn't show up at my home. The next evening, I was at my wits' end. My home was a mess, my children were sick, my son's hands were burnt, my hair, nails and feet were a mess, and I hadn't had any alone time with the hubby in weeks. I felt like I was losing it. I really felt like I was losing my mind. I sent text messages and made urgent calls, all in a plea for help, prayer and someone to talk me off of the ledge I wanted to jump off of so badly.

Days later I started waking up at 4 a.m. For three days in a row, I awakened without fail at 4 a.m. On the third morning, I realized that I wasn't awakened this way since I was praying and fasting trying to get pregnant two years earlier. I assumed God was trying to get my attention, so I began to pray. I also prayed for others who crossed my mind. I prayed for my husband, and my marriage, and I prayed for mothers all over the world who were dealing with babies born too soon. When I finished praying I read Romans chapters 9-11. I tried to get some rest afterwards, and the Holy Spirit whispered the scripture, Luke 12:48 *"To whom much was given, of him much will be required..."*

Not too much changed physically after that morning. The twins continued to get sick. We still had our share of hospital stays, battles against pneumonia, strep throat, ear infections and even Scarlet Fever, but spiritually I changed. God had given me *a peace that passed all understanding* and just like that, all was okay in the Langley home.

CHAPTER FOUR
GROWING PAINS

"To Whom Much Is Given Much Is Required." Luke 12:48

The twins had developmental issues. They had to have physical therapy, occupational therapy, cognitive therapy and speech therapy. Logan was always the faster out of the gate just as she had been out of the womb. David marched to the beat of his own drum. I wouldn't say he was slow, but he darn sure took his own sweet time. He didn't speak a complete coherent sentence until the age of four and they were few and far between. I hated when people would ask me, "What did he say?" School was hard for him initially. Hell, it was hard for me too. Every parent wants his or her children to achieve academically. For me, it seemed to be wishful thinking. David was given an IEP (Individualized Education Plan) when he started school, to receive services to accommodate his needs. Those services seemed to do little to provoke a desire in him to want to learn. He just didn't seem interested. Words spoken by his Pre-k 3 teacher one day seemed to have changed the trajectory of his desire to learn. They weren't encouraging words. She didn't speak well of his situation. In fact, she did just the opposite.

One day, before class began, David had to find his name on the board and place it under the posted day of the week. I watched him as he struggled. He had trouble spotting his own name among the host of other names on the board. His teacher, to no one in particular (I happened to be within hearing distance), said,

"I don't know why he is not getting it."

"He's just not keeping up with the rest of the class."

I was crushed. My son was crushed. He's always been sensitive, and I could see that his feelings were hurt. My reaction was swift and curt. I won't go into detail but needless to say, she was no longer his teacher. I quickly had him removed from her classroom.

David has been struggling with reading from the beginning. He was a micro-preemie for God's sake! We took all the necessary steps to prepare him for school. He had speech therapy, cognitive therapy, and occupational therapy. I had people coming to work with him at home at least three times a week. I read to him everyday. I spent hundreds of dollars on tools to help me help him. I prayed, and I fasted. I anointed his head with oil. I cried. I prayed some more. Nothing seemed to help change the way he was progressing. I couldn't get him to sit still long enough to master any skills. I fought with the school system to ensure that he had an IEP to receive the services that would help him along. I even started believing maybe it was more than developmental delays. I needed a reason for his "situation." I kept hearing his teacher's words. They were haunting me.

At one point, I stopped wanting him around other children his age. He was different, and it was starting to show. He didn't pronounce his words right. No one understood him when he spoke. I watched him listened and focus so intently during class, and yet, I knew his mind wasn't processing it all. I prayed and asked God to make a way. Help him Lord. Help him find his way.

One day while he played with his superhero action figures in his room, I heard him speaking. His voice was raised and animated. I went to his room to tell him to lower his voice, and when I got to the top of the steps I realized he was preaching. He had the chairs set up and had built a makeshift pulpit. I promise you it was like the windows of heaven had literally opened up for us. What I experienced that day was the beginning of another miracle.

Every day since (unless he's sick), David has preached a sermon. He prays by himself, with his family and for anybody that comes to his mind. With all his preaching, one would think that he would've been able to pick up reading. And yet, I was still waiting for him to read. I told him one day,

"You know you are going to have to read to understand the Bible."

He was encouraged but he still couldn't read. It just wouldn't click or stick.

The next year two years, we were blessed with a wonderful teacher. She worked with him really hard. She used all the tools available to her. She made sure he received every hour that was on his IEP for therapy. She worked with his therapists to ensure that he got it, but he was still far below grade level. His confidence was low, except for when he was preaching. I signed him up for extended school year throughout each summer. He was in a reading program and David still could not read. The summer going into second grade, I decided, I'm going to get a tutor. I couldn't do it anymore on my own. We needed some extra help. One of my clients referred someone that she had used previously for her daughter. Mr. B was God sent. He came to our house, did an evaluation and minced no words with my husband and me regarding his assessment of David. He started working with David twice a week at $50/hr. I didn't know how long I would be able to pay but I knew David was worth the sacrifice.

During his tutoring sessions, I would sit in the living room and listen. I would often hear him encouraging David. He would push him beyond his capacity. He started tutoring him a month before school started. His words were contrary to his Pre-K 3 teacher. I couldn't wait until David went back to school. I wanted his teachers and therapist to see his progress. We were starting fresh with a new teacher. When the school year started, David was issued the BOY (Beginning Of the Year assessment), and his results crushed me. He was reading on a level C. He should have been reading on level I. I thought, this couldn't be correct. There must have been a mistake. Memories of how his life had begun flooded my mind. Nothing ever came easy for him. He had struggled during every step of his life. He struggled to breathe. He struggled to sit up. He struggled to see. He struggled to walk. He struggled to speak. He struggled to read. He struggled to fit in. He struggled to live. His short life was so full of struggles. Why couldn't things just come easily for him, as they often did for his twin sister?

I showed his tutor the test results. I wanted to curse. We were paying a lot of money for tutoring and this boy still can't read. I was mad, I was sad, and I was scared. Every day after that assessment, his teacher would send me a text,

"Make sure David reads today, Mom."

Every day we read, he struggled. Two pages would take thirty minutes. He would cry, and so would I. In the car on our way to school one day, we prayed as we did every morning. I decided to speak very candidly to him. I said,

"David, I've done all I could do. It's up to you son. I've prayed. I've spent money. I've advocated for you to get the best help and services. You have to do it now. Mommy can't do it for you. You have to pray for yourself like you pray for everyone else and believe that God can help you. You are going to have to want to be a great reader. You have to believe in yourself. You can do it but you have to want to."

We prayed before they got out of the car, I anointed them with oil, and I went on with my day as I did everyday. I went home and didn't think much else of the morning conversation I had with David. That afternoon when he got home from school, David burst through the doors with the biggest smile.

"Guess what Mommy?"

What he said next helped increase my faith a little more.

"I'm reading on level F," he said.

When he reported to class that morning his teacher had retested him. This time was different, and his teacher told him he was now on level F. He went from a level C to a level F in less than a week. Prayers work.

I was excited but held back a little because I didn't know if this was fact. So I checked my emails and sure enough there was an email from his teacher explaining that they had in fact retested David and he was on level F. Still below but not far below. They retested him because his specialized instructor just couldn't believe that David could be that far below. She knew him and said that something had to have gone wrong during that first test. The favor of God was surely on this boy's life. And let me tell you, David has not stopped reading. He has been deliberate in his studies, pronouncing his words clearer and focusing while in class.

One night, I told him to read to his Dad and gave him a book titled "The Growing Tree." He read that book from start to finish with very little hesitation and when he came to a word he didn't know, he tapped it out, blended it together and read it perfectly. I could hear him reading from where I was in the bathroom, and I couldn't help but smile. Then, I heard his father beaming with pride say,

"Mommy, this boy is reading well in here," and my tears would not stop. I asked David what his goals were and he excitedly exclaimed,

"I'm going to be better than the best, and I'm going to be a preacher just like Bishop Owens."

"Yes, you are son. Yes you are."

Each year it seemed as if we had to face a new

storm. As soon as things got better for David, they started going badly for Logan. She was failing miserably in school. Because David struggled so hard in the beginning, we didn't focus too much on Logan and her academics. She always got good reports from school and she was meeting her milestones, but then came second grade, and it all went downhill.

She had some apprehensions about going to the second grade, almost as if she had some sort of premonition. She didn't want to be assigned to a particular teacher's classroom but wouldn't you know it- that's precisely what happened! She got the teacher she didn't want. I told her everything would be okay as long as she stayed focused and did her best she would be fine. My children are spoiled, and I've done all I could to keep them from disappointments, so I tried to have her transferred to another classroom. I told the administration about Logan's apprehension. They didn't move her and assured me that her teacher was experienced and worked well with children. She would do fine. Their reassurance couldn't have been further from the truth.

Second grade was an awful year for Logan. She seemed to be regressing. I panicked. I called a meeting with the administration and told them I wanted her tested. I expressed my concerns that I believed she wasn't connecting with her teacher. She was tested and nothing was found. The ophthalmologist changed the prescription in her glasses. Maybe she was having problems with her glasses. This new prescription might work. Nope, the new glasses didn't change a thing. It was time to bring in Mr. B again. I had him work with Logan. She was struggling, especially in math. The year came and went, and Logan continued to regress. I was determined that third grade would be different. We worked with flash cards, and I grilled her on her multiplication tables. We worked hard. Logan was different from David. She was stubborn, like me. If she didn't want to do something, she wouldn't do it.

It appeared that she was being lazy and stubborn so I started punishing her. There were days when I was so frustrated that I wanted to beat her, just as my mother would've done to me. But I couldn't. One evening when she was supposed to be reading I caught her asleep. I asked to see her homework and she confessed that she hadn't done it. I was furious. I told her to go upstairs and take off all her clothes. This was going to be the day that she got her first whipping.

I reflected on how hard I advocated for her to ensure that provisions were made to help her overcome her deficiencies. I was paying a tutor one hundred dollars a week to come to our home, and she wasn't willing to do her part. Oh yeah, she definitely deserved a beating. I went to my closet and retrieved a leather belt. The closer I got to her room, the more nervous I became. When I walked in her room, she was sitting on her bed naked from head to toe. I looked in her eyes and saw the worry. She was afraid. I saw myself. I saw my eight-year-old self, sitting on the bed nervously awaiting the inevitable. I couldn't do it. I loved her too much to hurt her. What was my spanking her with a belt going to change? I was so ashamed of myself. Ashamed that I was becoming everything I promised myself I wouldn't be to my children.

I instructed Logan to get dressed and I talked to her.

I asked questions and I let her answer. I listened. I tried to put myself in her shoes. I willed myself to understand what was happening from her point of view. After our talk, we prayed together and I told her I loved her. That night we did her homework together (minus my yelling). She continued to struggle a little in school, but she wasn't regressing as she was before and the best thing was she was trying. I kept the faith and prayed and believed God for what He had promised. Some days were rough. There were days I didn't want to get out of the bed. I was tired of meeting with teachers and administrators, and I didn't want to go to another doctor's appointment. I wondered how I was functioning day to day. It was God. I would not stop praying and believing God's word and believing all was well even when everything around me said it wasn't. I couldn't stop hearing my Bishops words,

"Don't lose your hope!"

Prayers prevailed and at the last award ceremony of the school year, both Logan and David received academic achievement awards. I couldn't have been more proud. They are thriving nine year olds. All of the challenges that they have faced from birth presented God the opportunity to show Himself. Today they rarely get sick. They have the occasional cold and Logan suffers with allergies, but we haven't had to go to Urgent Care all summer. David is below grade level in reading but he is a math wizard. Logan is the opposite. She still struggles in math, but she's on grade level and can read anything you put in front of her.

They aren't babies anymore but they are still my babies. Once again, God answered my prayers.

CHAPTER FIVE
LETTING GO

"Be anxious for nothing; but in everything by prayer and supplication with thanksgiving let your request be made known unto God." Philippians 4:6

Weddings, funerals and births bring out the worst or best in people. It seemed as if the birth of the twins brought out the best in my mother and my biological father. Around this time my biological father and I started forming a relationship. We talked on the phone often. I would see him when I went down south to visit relatives. He even came up to DC to visit a couple of times.

I released all the disappointment and resentment that I had towards my parents when I became a mother of my own children. When I became pregnant, I loved my unborn children with all that I had in me. I could not understand how anyone could go through life without having a relationship with his or her child. I was determined not to let history repeat itself with my kids. I was not my mother or father. I was a child of God, and I was destroying every generational curse and for a period of time things were going great between my father and me, and then it happened. The time came when I needed him, and he didn't show up again. This time was different. This time it wasn't about his neglect of me. It was about his neglect of my child. I needed him just like my son needed me.

David had been admitted into the PICU (Pediatric Intensive Care). For reasons that were never made clear, out of nowhere his head and face had begun to swell. He had become lethargic and had a bout of vertigo. His fever had reached 105.1. He was only three years old, and the doctors couldn't pinpoint the problem. We were in the hospital for an entire week. The doctors ran a bunch of test and did scans. They tried to do an MRI, but because he couldn't remain still, they weren't able finished the process and had to let him out of the machine. An intravenous drug therapy was started to treat him for a bacteria infection. He was in so much pain and was clearly suffering. I was at a lost. All I could do was hold him and pray. I prayed that my touch was enough to offer him some form of comfort. My father happened to be in town that week. He and my grandmother were visiting his sister and first cousin who lived in the area. His cousin, who was my second cousin, kept him abreast of what was going on with David. He called me and promised to come to the hospital the first chance he got.

A day went by and there was no sign of him. He

called again and said, “I’ll be over tomorrow.” Tomorrow came and he didn’t show up. He called me later that evening to let me know that he wouldn’t me able to visit. His mother was ready to go back home and he had to take her.

I was crushed. Whatever hope I had of us developing a father/daughter relationship that I, at onetime, use to dream about as a child, vanished in that last phone call. How could you not come visit your grandson who was in ICU? How could you not come to hug your daughter? How could you, a licensed minister, not come and pray with her and tell her everything would be all right? I decided that day that the only father I had and would ever have was my stepfather, James. I asked God to help me not hate him. I was ready to let go but I didn’t want to be angry or resentful this time. I wasn’t. I loved him and I needed him, but as usual he didn’t show up. The disappointment was deep and so was my hurt. I was done. If I never saw him again, it wouldn’t have mattered. I never mentioned him to my children, who at the time were too young to remember him. As far as they knew, the only granddaddy they had was my stepfather and I was good with it staying that way. Life went on and it was as if he never existed.

Around this time, my relationship with my mother was being strengthened. It was like the pregnancy and the birth of the twins caused some cosmic shift for the better in our relationship. We bonded over the twins. Initially, she was all in. It appeared that way for a while. Then she started not showing up for me. She was dealing with some personal things, and unfortunately those things prevented her from showing up when I needed her most. I tried to understand that she wasn't herself, that had she been herself she would have been there but it was hard.

One time in particular, really upset me. David had to have surgery to repair an inguinal hernia. He was only seven months. I was terrified for him. It would be his first time going under anesthesia. My mother had promised to meet me at the hospital the morning of his surgery. I had to be at the hospital at 5 a.m. so they could prep him for surgery. I sat in the waiting room anxiously awaiting my mother's arrival, but she never came. After hours of sitting nervously in the waiting room, the doctor came out to give me the good news of the surgery's success. I was elated at the news but disappointed that my mother wasn't there to share in my happiness or to support me. She didn't show up, and she didn't call. I tried calling her but she didn't answer my calls. David stayed overnight for observation, and I never once heard from her. I couldn't depend on my own mother.

Another time, I started a new job. The twins had gotten sick and I had to keep them home from school. I needed her to watch them. I hadn't been on the job long enough to use sick leave. She agreed. The next morning I packed up the twins and we headed to her house. Since I knew that my mother was a hard sleeper, I started calling her that morning before I started getting dressed. She didn't answer the phone. I figured that by the time I reached her house she would've been awaken by the constant ringing of her phone. I got to the front of her house and started honking my horn. I even got out of the car and yelled her name. There was no response. After about fifteen minutes, I left. I was left with no choice but to take the twins to work with me. Thankfully, neither of my supervisors came in that day, and no one knew that the children were at work with me. Once again, she let me down and I was so disappointed.

Disappointed became commonplace with my parents, but I was determined to be a better mother and parent to my children than they were to me. By this time, in my walk with Christ, I knew how it worked. If I prayed enough and if I fasted enough the pain I'd felt over the years would go away. The pain was still there. I was doing a pretty good job at masking my pain and my frustration. I was use to burying my feelings until I couldn't take it any longer and then I would unleash it in a fury of anger. It was always misdirected and misguided anger. Some poor, undeserving, and unsuspecting soul would be on the receiving end of my frustration. I didn't want to be that person any longer. There had to be an answer to my frustration.

My answer was to lower my expectations of people, my parents in particular. Sadly, I had to protect myself from disappointment. I stopped expecting them to show up. I no longer looked for them. Instead, I took a back seat to the relationships. I wanted them to chase me, to come after me as I had them all these years. I think at some point, my mom started to get it. My mom noticed but my father never did. It would be another six years before I heard from him again.

The thing was though, I was miserable. It wasn't who I was. For so long, I was the enabler in the relationships. I did whatever was necessary to make the relationships work. It had gotten to a point where I felt like

I was buying love and no matter how expensive it was I was willing to pay. But these were my parents. How could our relationship not work? I was their child. They were my parents. We had to have a relationship. Or did we? I had heard so many people talk about toxic relationships within families. But, as a person who loved family, letting my parents go was not going over well for me. It didn't matter that they were hurting me.

My children helped me to let go. They were noticing that my mother wasn't around often. One day David asked me why didn't granny ever answer her phone when we called. And my daughter wanted to know why we didn't visit her at her house anymore. I told them I didn't know. I suggested that they call their granny and express their feelings. I couldn't make excuses for her, and I couldn't let them think that I was the reason why they didn't see their granny regularly, especially since we only lived a five-minute car ride or fifteen-minute walk away from one another. I had to hold on to the hope that whatever issues my mom had that kept her from being all-in with her children and grandchildren, would eventually push her to get help. It was all I had. It was all I could do. I couldn't fix what I didn't break. It wasn't my fault. After years of feeling like I did something wrong, I just let them go. I let go of my father and I let go of my mother. I placed them in the care of a bigger presence than myself. I turned them over to God.

CHAPTER SIX
SEARCHING FOR KATE CARTER

"Ask, and it shall be given you; seek, and ye shall find; knock, and it shall be opened unto you." Matthew 7:7

My desire of wanting to belong to a large family raised my curiosity about my own extended family. My father came from a really large family but because he wasn't around I never got to know them. I was only close with one of my cousins on his side, and that didn't happen until I became an adult. I didn't really know anyone else. I knew of them and heard stories, but I didn't really know them. I wasn't raised around any of them, not even his other children. I never spent holidays or summers in any of their homes. My mother's family was small, and when I was a child, I spent a lot of time with them. It was nothing for my mother to awaken my sister and me in the middle of the night with a trip to Lynchburg. As small as my maternal side was, I didn't know too much about them either. My mother only shared snippets of her childhood. There was always a sad or angry undertone when she talked about the "good old days." We couldn't go back too far on the family tree. My grandmother was an only child. All I ever knew about my great-grandmother was that she had been raised in the home of a white family. I never heard anyone speak on anything else about her past. I didn't even know my grandmother's father. He and my great-grandmother weren't married when my grandmother was born. He was alive when I was a child and lived in the same neighborhood as my grandmother, but I never met him. I had never even heard of him until I was much older. As children, in my family, we didn't ask adults about their personal life. That was taboo. By the time I was of the age where I felt I was mature and comfortable enough to ask questions, my great grandmother had developed early stages of Alzheimer's disease. Any hopes I had of getting answers were now locked away in her slowly degenerating mind. My maternal grandmother was an only child. My maternal grandfather was the youngest of three brothers and was rumored to have had a sister, which no one ever met. My grandfathers siblings had all passed away at a young age, none had wives or children. My mother was the youngest of six children, so she didn't know much about my great-grandmother's life before she was born. I always wanted to know more about my great-grandmothers family but always came up empty when I started to ask questions. It was like her life before birthing my grandmother was a mystery. So I started doing my own research.

I had been a member of Ancestry.com since 2007. I started looking for anything that I could find on my great-grandmother. Initially, I kept coming up empty. I could only find her during the 1940's. She was born in or around 1906, so why couldn't I find anything on her until she was in her late thirties? After coming up short, I decided to give my research a break. I ended up breaking longer than I had intended.

This year, 2019, I became intentional in my searching. I got back on Ancestry and started doing some serious digging. I started searching the census reports and finally found my great-grandmother. I also found her mother. I had a name, I had a place of birth, and I even found my great-great grandmother's death certificate. I found Sarah Carter, my maternal great-great grandmother. I learned that my great-grandmother was not actually from Lynchburg, Virginia as I had originally thought, but she was in fact from Amherst, Virginia. This explained why I could not find her during my original search in 2002. I was searching in the wrong city. I was now intrigued, I didn't want to stop with Sarah Carter. I wanted to know where WE came from. I wanted to go back as far as I could before I hit the infamous brick wall. As one would expect, it's hard for descendants of African slaves to trace their history. Slave owners were very strategic in breaking up, breaking down and breaking apart the black family. Records such as birth certificates were not kept of people born into slavery. Sometimes the only record of a slave's existence was their listing as a number. No names. Maybe a scar, or a distinctive birthmark was used to describe them, but not a name. They were invisible except in the cotton or tobacco fields. If they were lucky or white enough, they may have had the honor of being a house nigger and not a field nigger. Their existence was simply for profit just as cattle.

I started hitting walls again. I couldn't find Sarah, my great-great grandmother's, family. Her death certificate had a Jesse Carter listed as her father, but her mother was listed as unknown. When I searched for Jesse Carter in Amherst, Virginia, I found several but couldn't narrow it down to which one could be her father. I first found my great-grandmother Kate with her mother Sarah, on the census taken in Amherst, Virginia. She was at the tender age of three-years-old. Much to my dismay, Kate's father was not listed. The generational curse of fatherless homes within our family had started. The 1910 Census listed them as living in a Poorhouse in Amherst, Virginia. They were listed as inmates. Imagine my surprise seeing that word...*Inmates*.

Did this mean my great-great grandmother, Sarah, was a criminal? Had she had my great-grandmother while she was in prison? Or did they lock her up after she had her child and force her to take the child with her to prison? I found one very interesting fact about my great-grandmother that I had never heard before now. She had siblings. In addition to her, there were three other children, one of which was listed as living with them in the Poorhouse. One of the children was deceased, it didn't say whether she had given birth to a stillborn or if the child had died sometime after, just that it was deceased. And the one child's whereabouts were unknown. There was no other information listed, and my continued search turned up nothing. The child listed, as living with them was a boy named Willie. Willie was six months old at the time of the census. Sarah was around the age of thirty-five. She was thirty-five and single with a three-year-old, a six-month-old, one deceased child and one child missing; living in a Poorhouse. There were no other Carters listed at the Poorhouse, so one could only assume that she was alone. What could have happened in her life that she would find herself in such dire straits? Where was her family? I kept asking myself over and over again, "Where is your family Sarah?"

I started doing research on Poorhouses, which were later called Almshouses, and learned that they often listed the inhabitants as inmates. The title was very misleading. They weren't actual inmates. Most people who lived in Poorhouses or on Poor Farms were impoverished with no means of caring for themselves. They usually did not have family, and if they did, their family didn't or wasn't able to care for them. Sarah lived in the Poorhouse for over 30 years, and according to her death certificate, died at the Poorhouse and was buried at the Poorhouse cemetery as a pauper.

The Poorhouse or Almshouse, as they were sometimes called, doesn't exist today. Apparently, neither do any of the records for the Amherst County Poorhouse. In my extensive research, I came up empty-handed after 1928. I'd even gone to the courthouse in the town of Amherst to do research, only to hit another brick wall. According to the 1920 census, Sarah was still living in the Poorhouse or on the Poor Farm, as it was called by then, but Kate and Willie were no longer with her. I did find Kate on the 1920 census but she was no longer with her mother Sarah. She was thirteen years of age living with the Walkers, a white family, in the Court House District of

Amherst, Virginia. She was listed as their servant. How she got there was anybody's guess. And how long she was there was just as mysterious. I don't know if she was legally adopted, stolen or sold. I just know that ten years after finding her with her mother at the age of three in a poorhouse, she's now, at the age of thirteen, living in a house with strangers and listed as their servant. This saddened me. Was she mistreated? Did they ever tell her who and where her mother was? I assumed not, since she never spoke of it to her family.

Poor Willie, I was never able to find what happened to him after 1910. He was only six months at the time. Was he adopted, sold or stolen? Was he living with someone that changed his name? Did Sarah's family come and get him from the Poorhouse? Was he still living in 1920? As for the third living child, I never did find information on them. I was told that my great-grandmother had a sister name Alice, but Alice didn't have any children. During my research, I've never been able to confirm that Alice was her actual sister. I was hitting brick wall after brick wall in my search, so I decided to do DNA testing through Ancestry, hoping that somehow there were descendants of Sarah also looking for family members.

I ordered the test and received it a week later. I followed the directions and eagerly gave up my DNA by spitting in a tube and mailing it off to a lab. I anxiously awaited the results. Within a week I received an alert via email that the DNA had been received and it would take about six to eight weeks before I received the results. I wasn't sure if I would get any DNA matches. After all, my mom's family was tiny. My nervous anticipation came to a climax on March 15, 2019. That was the day I received the email that my DNA results were in, and I must say I was pleasantly surprised. I had no idea that I would get as many matches as I did. Yes, I was excited about knowing my heritage history and what region on the vast continent of Africa my ancestors were stolen from, but I was more interested in the actual persons who were a match with my DNA. There were over 900 matches. Two of those were first cousins, and two were second cousins. I found my great-grandma Kate's family! Or did I? Maybe these were my father's family.

First cousins. I was excited. I clicked on each match, and carefully searched through his or her family trees. There was so much information. There were so many names to search. As I searched one thing became clear right away, none of these matches were Carters, Smiths or Whites. I thought that maybe Carter was Sarah's married name. Perhaps she married at some point and her name changed. But then I remembered her death certificate and it had her father listed as Jesse Carter, so Carter had to have been her maiden name. Then I started wondering, "How could I have a first cousin that I didn't know?" I knew all of my maternal cousins. And yes, due to my father's absence, I didn't know many of my paternal cousins. I knew my paternal aunt's children, but I didn't know any of my paternal uncles children. I did know the surnames of my father's family and I didn't recognize the last names that I was seeing on Ancestry. My father's family was largely Smiths as was my mother's family. I didn't recognize any of the surnames that I matched. And so, my curiosity was piqued.

One of the first cousins on Ancestry had a profile picture and after studying the picture, I thought that he favored my great-grandma Kate. Same face, lips, and eyes. I decided to reach out to him. I sent him a message through Ancestry, and to my surprise, he replied immediately with a phone number. I didn't call right away because to be quite honest, I was a little nervous. I was getting so close to finding my maternal family. I called after about a week, and after playing phone tag for a couple of days, we finally spoke. It was magical. I know this may come across as corny and weird, but we instantly connected. It didn't feel as though I was talking to a stranger. Any nervousness I had went out the window at "Hello." It was like talking to someone that I had known my whole life, like a big brother. We couldn't figure out how and why our DNA match was so strong, but we both knew that we were blood. There was no denying it.

He told me he was on Ancestry looking for his great-grandfather on his maternal side whose surname happened to be Smith, just like my maternal granddaddy, and was piecing together history on his paternal side. I told him about my maternal search. The interesting part was his family and my great-grandmother all were from the same city in Virginia. On top of that, some of them had even relocated to Lynchburg, Virginia, just as my great-grandmother Kate had done so many years ago. This had to be the connection! I felt like Alex Haley during an episode of Roots. I found my family! I was so excited to share this information with my mother. She was excited too until I revealed the surnames of the people with whom I had the DNA matches. I couldn't help but notice the excitement in her voice dwindled just a little.

My cousin, Delando was his name, thought it would be a good idea for me to go to his Facebook page and look at pictures of his family. Just to see if I would recognize anyone or see any resemblances. I did that and some of the faces stood out for me. Not only were the faces familiar but also so was the statue. Let me explain, I'm short. My great-grandma was short, and so was my grandma. When I say short, I'm talking 5'2 and less, short. There were a lot of short people in his family, and again, I started getting excited. I'd definitely found Kate Carters family! I came across one picture in particular that drew me in more. It was a picture of three men, and they were my cousin's uncles. I found out that they were all brothers. There was something about one of the brother's eyes that made me want to learn more about him. So I clicked on his name to view his Facebook page. Once on his page, I could clearly see that he was short, just like my grandma and great-grandma. Just like me. Each picture I saw of him looked as if his eyes were looking directly into my eyes. I took a screenshot of his picture and sent it to my mother. Do you remember that fateful March day that I spoke of earlier? Well, this was that day.

"Mommy, doesn't he look like your grandmother?"

I asked.

She didn't respond right away but when she did her reply was, "Hmm."

I spoke with my cousin several times in the following month, and he decided that it would be good for me to speak with one of his Aunts. Perhaps she could help us put some of the pieces to the puzzle together. She had after all lived in both Amherst and Lynchburg. We scheduled a day and time for the conversation which ended up happening the first week of May. Again, I was nervous because I didn't know whether this would lead to another dead end or whether I would open up Pandora's box. True to his word, my cousin called on the day and time that we scheduled, and he had his aunt on the line. Initially, she was curt, and I was a little thrown off by her tone.

"Baby let me just tell you now, you are no relation to us," she said.

I laugh when I tell the story now, but I didn't laugh that day. I was known for having a smart mouth but I wasn't the angry little girl that I was before, I was now changed. I refrained from saying something smart for several reasons, but the number one reason was, Nancy taught me well. I was to respect my elders. I did think her initial response was rude, but I got over it because I wanted to find out more information. My cousin had to reiterate to her that DNA linked us. We all know that DNA doesn't lie. People lie, but DNA not so much.

She asked me questions about my family, and I explained that my family did not live in Amherst, they never did, only my great-grandmother and her mother were from Amherst, everyone else was born and raised in Lynchburg, Virginia. She told me that she too was raised for a while in Lynchburg. As the conversation progressed, we discovered she not only lived in Lynchburg but that she actually lived in the same neighborhood and on the same street as my family. She asked my parents name, and I told her, Nancy and Peewee. Upon learning my parent's identity, she revealed that not only did she know my parents, but also she and my mother at one time, were best friends. Her tone changed and I was getting lost in the conversation. Her voice softened and she seemed apologetic. Although at one time she, without reservation, denounced my kinship, she now readily agreed that we were related- even if she didn't know how. Perhaps through my father's side we were related. Everybody is related when you come from these small country towns.

How many of you have experienced the joy and dismay of going on a rollercoaster ride? First you experience the excitement. You stand in the long line waiting for your chance to board the car and get securely strapped in your seat. You nervously pull on the harness to make sure it's secure. You receive instructions, keep your hands in the car, don't stand while the ride is moving, and secure all of your belongings. The ride takes off, and everyone is happy. You hold your hands up as it makes its first up hill climb.

This part of my story is likened unto a rollercoaster ride. I'm on the part where you are going up the incline. I'm anticipating the first drop, I'm too amped up to be scared. Up and up and up. And the closer to the top I get the more nervous I am. I start to realize that this ride was a stupid idea. I'm not really a fan of rollercoaster rides. I should've never gotten on this thing in the first place. But its too late, I'm on it. It's nearing the top. I've been warned about trying to disembark once the ride has started. After all, the drop is steep. If I get off now, I will surely meet my demise. I close my eyes and pray to God the ride doesn't malfunction while I'm on it and that I make it safely to the end. My gut told me that I was in for one hell of a ride.

CHAPTER SEVEN
HIS PURPOSE

"Many are the plans in a man's heart, but it is the Lord's purpose that prevails." Proverbs 19:21

After hanging up with my cousin and his aunt, my cousin calls me back. I think at this point we both knew that there was more to be revealed. We knew we had stumbled upon something big, but we didn't know how big. We promised to keep searching and to keep each other abreast of whatever we found. I called my mom with the news.

"Guess who I talk to today?" I said to my mother.

"Who?" She asked.

"Cookie, Cookie Mays," I replied. "She said you all were best friends as teenagers."

I'm sure the silence only last a couple of seconds

but I swear it felt like it took ten minutes for my mother to respond.

"Yes, I know and remember Cookie," she said. I thought this was strange but I continued,

"I've never heard you mention her."

Again, silence. She finally got around to asking me what we talked about and I explained how Cookie was my cousin's aunt and how he had set up the phone call so that we could have a conversation about our families. I jokingly said that she and her long lost best friend might actually be cousins.

"Wouldn't that be something?" I asked.

"Indeed it would," was her response.

We talk a little more and then said our goodnights. It wasn't until after the call that the queasiness you get from a rollercoaster ride came back. No matter what I did, the feeling wouldn't let up. I was now at the top of the track. One half of the coaster was hanging down and the other half was coming up and over. It's too late to get off. I can't stop it. It starts to drop, and it's dropping fast.

That night was restless, I tossed and turned all night. I got up at one point during the night and pulled up my cousin's Facebook page. I started going through his pictures again. I found what I was looking for, the reason I couldn't sleep. It was the gentleman that I saw before, the one whose picture I had sent to my mother months earlier. There they were, his eyes staring at me, piercing my heart. He was watching me. I tried to shake what I thought. There was something in his eyes that belong to me. I needed to find out what it was, and more importantly, who he was.

The next morning, I called my mother. We had a date to visit the National Archives to do more research on Sarah and Kate. She didn't answer. This isn't unusual because she rarely answers her phone, but she will call back. This time she didn't. I called her all day. No answer. Each time she didn't answer, the rollercoaster rushed down the drop faster. I started to feel sick. It seemed as though the drop was never-ending. I called my cousin, we talked for a while, and I shared some of my thoughts. He understood and like a big cousin, promised to help me through whatever happened. We were family. I called my sister to see if she had heard from my mother. My sister is younger than me by three years, but she's always been able to remain calm whenever I'm having a moment. This was a moment.

"Amy, mom is embarrassed and ashamed," she said, "She's probably afraid to face you."

In my naivety or denial, I asked, "Afraid of what?"

What she says next rocked me to my core and would change my life forever,

"Peewee is not your father."

The rollercoaster is now dropping at full speed. My eyes are closed, and I don't see the bottom.

"The picture you sent mom a couple of months ago, that man is your father."

The rollercoaster is now dropping into a black tunnel. Remember the movie, *Empire Strikes Back*, when Dark Vader revealed that he was Luke's father? Or the movie, *Antoine Fisher*, when he finally found his family? Or *The Color Purple*, when Pa was not Pa? I felt like I was living through each one of those scenes in that one moment. Yet, in typical Amy fashion, I toughened up. I put on a brave face and acted as if everything was okay. I assured my sister that I was fine. It was such a long time ago. My mother was only sixteen when she discovered she was pregnant with me. I couldn't and wouldn't hold against her a decision she made at sixteen. I loved her. Love covers a multitude of sins. I hung up with my sister and then I cried. Next, I called my cousin.

"I think one of your uncles is my father," I said, as I stared at the picture of his uncle that I had saved on my phone.

"Really, which one do you think it is?" he asked me.

I told him about the conversation I had with my sister and shared what she said about Pee Wee not being my dad.

He asked me how I was feeling and I realized that I hadn't had time to process my feelings. I didn't know how I felt. He assured me with his words, "I got you cousin," and "I'm rocking with you to the end."

He began to tell me a little about his uncle. He was a family man. He had a wife and four daughters, and he was a Pastor. The last statement did something. Really, my dad was a Pastor? We talked some more and he told me to check my phone because he had sent me some pictures.

"If my Uncle Darnell is your father, these are your sisters," he said.

I looked at those pictures and almost dropped my phone. The similarity was unmistakable. It was like looking at pictures of myself. I knew it without knowing it; the man with the eyes, was my biological father. All of this took place outside of my friend's hair salon, where I was waiting for another friend as she got her hair done. In a span of three to five minutes, I cried, I laughed and I prayed. I had so many feelings that I suddenly went numb. I didn't know what to feel. Should I be angry or happy? Should I be pissed at my mother or pissed with my biological father. I didn't know the story so I didn't know how to feel. All I knew for sure was that my life from that point on was about to change.

I didn't know what to do, so I went inside my girlfriend's salon and just showed my two friends a picture of one my sisters. They both looked at the photo and shrugged their shoulders. They thought it was a picture of me except younger. When I told them what I had just learned they were in disbelief. I joked about it a little, and we went on with the day.

I called my stepdad next and gave him the news. I wanted to know if he knew. He was shocked and I could tell by his reaction, he didn't know. He was very comforting, asking me how I felt and assuring me that he would help me get through another poignant moment in my life. As always, he was there. He had always been. It then hit me. How could I possibly be happy about this discovery? So many people would be affected. My mother, Peewee, my stepfather, my biological father, his wife, his children, my children, my husband, all would be affected by my discovery. What had I done?

I sent the picture of one of my sister's to my husband. He called and asked why did I send a picture of myself. I told him the story. His response wasn't what I needed at that time. He told me to leave it alone.

"James is your father," he said, "and if I was you I would leave well enough alone."

But all wasn't well and I couldn't and wouldn't leave it alone. I needed to see my father's eyes in person. I needed him, and a part of me felt like he needed me too.

I still had not heard from my mother so I sent her a text:

"*Good Morning. I love you, and I commend you for your strength. You were young and afraid. You raised a beautiful, intelligent and curious daughter. It was only fitting that I would find out because you know I'm nosey, LOL. Seriously, I'm not mad or disappointed. God saw fit to orchestrate things the way He did and it's okay. Please don't isolate yourself from me because I am not upset. Just know that it's been me and you since you were pregnant at the age of 16 and it will always be us.*"

She didn't respond to the text. It wasn't until later that night around 9 o'clock p.m., that she called and asked if we could talk in person. The next morning, after dropping off the twins to school, I picked her up, and we went to breakfast. I could tell by her posture that she was apprehensive as she walked towards the car. I smiled to reassure her that all was well.

"I'm sorry, I didn't know," she said as she got in the car. I told her that I believed her, although I was unsure. The ride to breakfast was tense. We lightheartedly chattered not really sure of how to start the conversation.

I finally asked, "Is the guy in the picture my father?"

"Yes, his name is Marshall," she said, "but I knew him as Darnell." She wasn't looking at me as she spoke.

"He doesn't know he's your father."

"So he doesn't know about me?" I asked, still in disbelief that any of this was occurring.

"No, he doesn't," she said.

"He was a really nice guy," she said as she began to tell me about their short-lived romance or rendezvous that resulted in my birth. She said at the time they hooked up she was dating and in love with my father, Peewee. When she found out she was pregnant, she thought that there was no way she could have been pregnant by anyone other than Peewee.

Now every since I can remember, my mother has always told me that Peewee was her first love and first sexual partner. She told me that she had gotten pregnant the first time she had sex with him. Perhaps she used that story as a scare tactic for me not to have sex, but it's definitely the story that was etched in my mind. Now I know that wasn't even close to the truth.

After further discussion about Marshall, we agreed that he deserved to know that he had a child, albeit an adult child. She asked me to allow her reach out to him and deliver the news, and I agreed that would best. I didn't know him and I definitely wasn't going to pop up on his doorstep or worse, show up at one of his church services or at his job.

My mom and I had our coming to Jesus moment on Tuesday, May 7th. Every day after that was agonizing. I couldn't sleep. All kinds of scenarios would play in my head. What if he rejected me? What if his wife and children rejected me? To reject me was to reject my children and what about my children? Do I tell them now or do I wait until I've met him? I think I lost a couple of pounds during that wait time because I had lost my appetite. I told myself that I would give my mother a couple of weeks to make things right.

My church was having a for ladies only twelve-week bible study every Monday night at 7 p.m. The day I discovered the news of my biological father happened to be the same day that the bible study began. The second week after my mother's confession, I went to bible study as planned. I arrived early. I sat in my car stalking my biological father's Facebook page. I looked at pictures with he and his wife, his children and grandchildren. I looked at pictures of him in the pulpit. I tried to see if I saw me. As I was perusing his page, my mom sent me a text:

"I reached out to Marshall. No response thus far."

My worst nightmare was becoming more of a reality. I was being rejected. My mind was racing, he doesn't want anything to do with me, I thought. I responded back to her saying, *"Leave it alone. I don't feel like any more disappointments."*

I threw my phone in my purse, gathered my things and got out of my car. I needed to be in the presence of God and other sisters-in-Christ. I'm not sure what I would have done in that moment if it weren't for bible study. I was trying so hard to hold it together, but my eyes kept watering, as I fought back tears, and I felt like I was getting a migraine. My phone rang as soon as I entered the sanctuary. It was my cousin.

"Hello."

"Hey cousin, how you been?" he said, "I haven't heard from you, is everything okay?"

I told him about my mom's text. I also said something about wishing I hadn't uncovered what I did. I guess he could sense my heaviness and he reassured me that "we" would get through it together and that no matter what, we were family.

Getting through bible study that night was hard. I cried for nothing and prayed silently through most of the class. I prayed that I wouldn't be rejected. The devil kept playing with my head and bringing up old feelings of not being good enough. I always felt like an outsider in Peewee's family, never feeling as if I fit. I was never really welcomed into the family of the person that I once knew as my father. His mother never embraced me like most grandmothers embrace their grandchildren. His sister and I lived one state away from each other and I can count on two fingers how many times she reached out to me. He had a huge family and only one member of the family had ever made me feel like family and that was my cousin Kimberly. Kimberly is actually Peewee's first cousin, but you wouldn't know she wasn't my first cousin if we didn't tell you. We had been thick as thieves for the last 10 years or so. My kids love her and she loves them. Realizing that she was not my blood sadden me. The thought made me cry even harder that night.

My cousin sent a text during class asking me to call him as soon as possible. He had some news to share with me. Class ended and before I could call him, he called me.

"Hey cuz, what did you pray about tonight?" he asked.

I could sense some excitement in his voice. I can't recall my response but the next thing he said to me stopped me in my tracks.

"Your dad wants to talk to you," he said. "I told him I would call you on the three way, is it okay?"

It took me a second before I heard myself say,

"Yes, give me a chance to get in my car."

Once I got in the car, he put me on hold and dialed the number. The next voice I heard was that of my father. Hearing his voice made me cry, but his words were what opened up the floodgates.

"I am so sorry," he said.

"You are my daughter and I am your father," he told me. "And no matter what anybody says or does, I accept you as my child."

We talked until I arrived home. We both shared as much as we could about ourselves in that little time. He told me that I had four sisters. One with whom I'm the same age for about six months. I'm his oldest. We both cried. I think my cousin may have even cried. He told me that he had, in fact, received messages from my mother about me being his child and that initially, he was angry. This explained why she never heard a response from him. He was processing everything. After all, he hadn't seen my mother in 48 years. He told me that he shared with his wife and decided he needed to speak with me directly. I'm glad he did. It made the difference. He asked me to lead prayer before we got off of the phone. That sealed it for me because only my real daddy could have known how important prayer was to me.

I sat in the car for thirty minutes after that initial call. I probably cried for twenty-nine of those thirty minutes. Once I got myself together, I went into the house to share with my husband. For whatever reason, when I entered the house I didn't share as I intended. Instead, I went in my closet and prayed. I gave God thanks. As I shared earlier, nothing for me comes easy. And I knew that my enemy, the devil, wasn't going to let this story end as a fairytale.

CHAPTER EIGHT
THE TRUTH OF THE MATTER

"And ye shall know the truth, and the truth shall make you free." John 8:32

The next morning I got a text which said, "I love you Amy." It was the first text I received that day. It was from Marshall. I've gotten the same text every day since our first phone call. It's what he does for those he loves. Every day he sends a text with well wishes and love. I hadn't spoken to him for a couple of days since our initial conversation. I hadn't told my mom that we were in contact. I wasn't sure how she was going to react. I didn't want her to be angry with me. I don't know why I thought she would be angry, but I did. I didn't want her to feel like I was choosing him over her. I needed her to know that I was loyal. Good, bad or indifferent she was still my mother.

One morning coming home after dropping the twins

off to school, he was heavy on my heart. I prayed really hard for him and his wife. Not knowing anything of their family life, I knew I didn't want to be the cause of any strife in their marriage. I thought it would be best for us to do a DNA test. A DNA test would shut the mouths of any naysayers, and to be honest it would give me the closure and peace that I needed. A DNA test would be best for everyone involved. He called me at that moment. It was the second time I heard his voice since finding out about him. We spoke about the DNA test and decided that he would find a place for us to have it done. I was willing to go to Lynchburg. Whatever the day and time, I was going to be there for the test. He called me the next day with the scheduled day and time.

I had only told a couple of friends about my revelation. I made the decision to wait until the DNA results came in before I made it public. There was still a small chance that he wasn't my dad. He had two living brothers and as far as I was concerned, anyone of them could have been my father. My friend, Rickia, one of the few friends that I had shared my new discovery with, was so excited about the news that she couldn't wait to go visit him.

"Okay, when are we going?" she asked.

"Oh, you wanna ride with me?"

"Girl, yes, I'm riding with you," she said, "I can't wait to meet Uncle Pastor"

I was trying to think of who I needed to be there and who would want to be there and only a couple of people came to mind. Out of the few people I wanted to go, Rickia was one of them and she happened to be the only one that was able ride. I didn't even tell my husband what I was planning to do that day. I didn't want any pushback or negativity. We met Marshall in Charlottesville, Virginia at Noon.

Do you believe in love at first sight? Have you ever met someone for the first time and felt as if you've known him or her your whole life? That was my experience the first time I met Marshall. Pulling into Charlottesville, initially my nerves started to get the better of me. However, when he pulled into the parking lot and got out of the car, all nervousness disappeared. This was my daddy. I could tell by his stride. His gait was one of confidence. As he got closer, I saw it in his eyes. I was looking at myself. There they were, the eyes from the pictures on Facebook. It wasn't some kind of mirage. He was actually looking at me. Taking all of me in, as I was he. We both knew, but we went through the technicalities anyway.

As we set inside the facility waiting for our names to be called, we chatted. I jokingly said, "The worst that could happen is that you aren't my dad but at least you will be my uncle."

He didn't find that funny.

We ended the day with lunch, the three of us- him, Rickia, and me. We had good conversation, and I felt so at ease with him. I even kissed him on his baldhead. I quickly learned we both shared a love for coffee. I studied him closely as I saw myself in his eyes. We have very similar mannerism. It was like God had taken forty-eight years to give me a present. It was a present that was mine, but that I was neither ready nor prepared to receive before that day. After lunch, it was time for us to part ways. I needed to get home before my husband and children started to wonder about my whereabouts. I missed him as soon as we pulled out of the parking lot. He called me several times before I reached home to make sure we were okay on the road. It was a strange and surreal ride home. I couldn't believe that I had just finished breaking bread with my dad. In a span of a couple of weeks, I had prayed and broken bread with my real daddy.

Nothing was left to do but wait for the results of the test. We waited, and while we waited we bonded. Since meeting in Charlottesville, we talked every single day. He told me a lot about himself. Some things were not too pleasing, especially since he was a pastor. His love for God and the things of God at such a young age reminded me so much of my son David and ironically enough, some parts of his life were very similar to that of King David. My son David had started preaching ever since he started speaking. As a matter of fact, when he preached, his voice was clear and so was his diction, more so than when he spoke. David declared at a young age, around five years old that the Lord told him he was going to be a preacher. Although I was saved and had been for a while, I often wondered where he got his passion. He had always been so on fire for God. Now it all started to make sense. Preaching was a part of his bloodline. It was in his DNA.

My father and I began to video chat. Our conversations sometimes included his wife, who seemed nice enough. I still hadn't told my children about him, and I didn't bring him up in conversations with Bernard. I wanted to have proof. I wanted concrete evidence. As the days passed, the enemy started creeping into my thoughts again. Each day we waited, the devil continued to play with my thoughts. I started thinking of all of the “What ifs?”

“What if he’s not my father?”

“What if the test somehow got mixed up with someone else’s?”

“What if one of his brothers is my father?”

“What if his wife hates me?”

“What if my children don’t like him?”

“What if they don’t understand?”

“What if his other daughters don’t like me?”

It was Tuesday, the fourth of June when I received the confirmation and proof that I had been anxiously awaiting. Marshall Darnell Mays was my biological father. I learned that day that my father was just as dramatic as I and so the reveal of the results was no less drama-filled than should’ve been expected. Neither of us was technologically savvy and the results were sent via email to his email address. Trying to open the attachment that held the results was both hysterical and exhausting. He texted me, “*Call me.*” I called him and he answered sounding out of breath as if he had been running.

“I got the results,” he said nervously, “but I can’t open the attachment.”

After a bunch of text messages back and forth and missed calls, he finally called and said that he was finally able to open the email attachment. After several unsuccessful attempts at opening the email, he decided to solicit help from the front desk clerk at the hotel where he was staying.

He asked me did I want him to read me the results. I wanted to scream,

"Read the damn results!"

But I wouldn't dare. My mother taught me better. So I held my peace. My nerves were getting the best of me as he prolonged and dragged out the reveal…purposely.

"It says, Marshall Mays can not…" I stopped him.

"Wait, you aren't my father?" I asked.

Now my nerves were really shot. I had been conversing with this man for the past month. We had bonded. I was so sure. How could he not be my father?

"Do you want me to read the rest?" he asked.

I didn't, but I said yes.

"Marshall Mays CAN NOT be excluded as the father," he said. "I am 99.9999% your daddy!" he said excitedly.

"You found your daddy!"

My rollercoaster ride had suddenly come to a complete stop. I was able to disembark. I had made it, and I was alive. I survived the ride. I felt one hundred pounds lighter. I didn't realize until that moment, just how much I had been carrying. Tears started to fall down my face. I couldn't help but to keep our conversation brief. I needed to regroup. I needed to tell God thank you. I needed to be alone, just God and me. I didn't call him back that day. I said I would, but I didn't. I was too overwhelmed. The next morning, I called my mother with the good news.

She said, "Damn."

"Damn." That was the response I got from my mother. It wasn't what I expected, and it sure wasn't what I needed, but that was my mother, always unpredictable. I shouldn't have expected anything more, but I did. I thought she would've at least shown some compassion. I was coming to grips with the fact that I had a father that actually cared about me and belonged to me. Questions I had about my ways and my personality were being answered in such a short period of time. I knew my discovery meant she would have to face some truths, but I thought that maybe just this once, she would put me and my feelings before her own. She didn't. She started talking about how she would have to move from her new home. She had just gotten settled into her new life in Lynchburg and now it was being disrupted. She didn't want anyone else to find out about my discovery. My discovery was sure to change the lives of many. She would become the talk of the town. To me she sounded like a narcissist. It was about her…again.

Lynchburg, the city of seven hills, is a small city located in Central Virginia. The black community within the city is even smaller. Gossip is a part of the community, as it is with many other communities just like it. Everybody knows somebody that has had my same experience. There are more secrets and lies within the community she grew up in that it's a shame. I heard stories growing up about incest, broken homes, abuse and yes, even questionable paternities. She wasn't the first, and she surely wouldn't be the last. I couldn't understand why she didn't see that. It happened forty-eight years before, shucks almost forty-nine. I had forgiven her for her part. I needed her to let me have my moment. I was happy, the happiest I had been in a while, and she was ruining it for me big time. She was blowing my high, so to speak. Why did she have that effect on me? More importantly, why did I allow her to have that effect on me?

Perhaps she didn't want to face it because she had known all along. Did she really know? She said she didn't.

The physical similarities I shared with my dad were far more noticeable than they had been with Peewee. We were both short. I had his eyes and his nose. The resemblance was strikingly familiar. How could she not have known? I didn't look anything like Peewee. She had to have seen some of Marshall Mays when she saw me. Did she leave Lynchburg because she didn't want to be exposed? These were questions that rested on my heart. And since I knew that I would never present those questions to her, I had to turn it over to God. None of it was my fault. I had to accept what God had allowed for me. I couldn't change the past, and I wasn't responsible for my mother's decisions. I had to walk in the steps that were ordered for me.

Now that I knew the truth, what were my next steps? I decided to tell my husband and my children. This time my husband was a tiny bit more receptive. Initially he worried about me and how I would be affected. He's never wanted to see me hurt. My husband is very protective of our children and me. He had more than once unselfishly put his life and reputation on the line for me. I knew that he had a close bond with my stepfather. I didn't want him to feel as if he had to choose between my stepfather and my father. I allowed him space and didn't try to force it on him. Once he saw the immediate bond that my biological father and I developed he was more accepting of the idea that yes, this is her dad.

My children were amazing. They asked questions, and I answered as best I could. It was important for me not to keep secrets from them. I answered honestly without making anyone look bad. I told them the truth. They loved their granny, my mother, and they loved their granddaddy, my stepdad. I wanted to make sure they understood that nothing was changing except that their family was growing considerably. They were excited and couldn't wait to meet their new family. I made plans to visit. It would be the first visit after receiving the DNA results.

The day the results came back, I received three Facebook notifications. All three were welcoming me into the Mays family. The first was from his wife, my stepmother Florence, who I affectionately call, Auntie Ma. The other two were from my sisters, Silisa and Catoria. None of them could've understood how much their small gestures of kindness meant to me. My relationship with them grew leaps and bounds since that day. My stepmother, God bless her, is a living example of the Proverbs 31 virtuous woman.

Next, I told my stepdad. I had told him my initial findings, but I never told him about meeting my dad or taking the DNA test. I didn't tell him because I felt in some way I was being disloyal. I didn't think I was right for loving another dad or even calling another man daddy. I've always called my stepdad by his first name and he deserved to be called dad. I've never called anybody dad not even Peewee. My stepfather was everything a little girl could dream of in a father. He was kind and attentive. He was thoughtful and caring. He taught me so much about life. He explained to me the facts of life. He could have walked away when he and my mom divorced, but he didn't. He had always been consistent and constant. He helped me purchase my first two cars. He was the one that moved my furniture out of the house when I left my first husband. He kept me out of jail. He got me back in school when the principal wanted to expel me for fighting. He walked me down the aisle as I married the love of my life. He was there for the birth of my children. My stepdad was always there, and in that moment, I felt as if I was betraying him. Betraying him because I wanted to call someone else daddy, something I had never called him. For once, I had to put myself first.

I hesitantly told him. I don't know how he felt at that moment, but if he felt anything other than happiness for me, he didn't show it. I hoped he wasn't just "putting on" for me. After talking about the situation several times with him, I was convinced he was genuinely happy for me. I mentioned to him how disinterested my husband had been initially and how bad it made me feel and how I thought it had something to do with him. It was my thought that my husband hadn't wanted my stepfather to feel slighted. My stepdad told me that he didn't feel slighted. He wanted for me what every father wants for their child, to be loved and at peace. I deserved it. He knew who he was in my life and nothing and no one would or could change who we were to one another. He was even willing to ride to Amherst with me one day. He wanted to meet my dad. My stepfather has always been that kind of man, void of selfishness. I never noticed a selfish bone in his body. I'm eternally grateful that God allowed his and my mother's paths to cross. When he fell in love with my mother, he fell in love with her daughters. God gifted me with the best dad in the world at just the right time in my life.

I began sharing the news with family and friends and everybody was receptive and happy. But I couldn't shake the feeling that somebody was being left out of the celebration and after praying about it; I realized it was my absent dad, Peewee, as most people called him. I hadn't heard from him in about six years, since David was last released from ICU. At first, I felt like it wasn't my place to tell him. I mean I wasn't his baby mama. I was the victim in all of this. It wasn't my fault. It was my mother's job to tell him and not mine. But as each day passed, I couldn't stop thinking about the situation or him. Right was right. I wanted to call him but against my better judgment, I continued to put it off for another day. "It's not my business to tell him," I kept telling myself, "it's my mothers." She had promised me that she would.

One day I got a call letting me know that the news of my discovery was being talked about in Lynchburg. It's hard to keep news from spreading in a small town like Lynchburg. There was no way I was going to allow this to get out of control. There would be no rumors and no lies on my watch. I was not going to allow my mother to bear the brunt of my discovery as if it were such an awful thing, so I did what I thought was best. I called Peewee and I told him myself. I told him everything from the beginning. I told him about Ancestry about the test. And when I finished telling him, I told my other siblings, his children. Nothing would change for me where they were concerned. I was still their big sister.

What my father, Peewee, revealed to me in our conversation totally messed up my head. HE ALREADY KNEW. Yes, you read it right, he knew. His mother had told him about six years prior.

"Really?" I asked.

"Well why in the hell didn't he tell me?"

He said that his mother told him that it was rumored that I wasn't his daughter and that Marshall was in fact my father. I then wondered was that the reason he didn't come see David in the hospital? After all, it had been about six years since David had taken ill and was in ICU.

How long had his mother known? She must have been holding on to that secret for a long time. Why had she chosen to release the information when she did? I was at least forty-one or forty-two when she told him. Perhaps that was why she never treated me as if I was her grandchild. She wasn't mean towards me but she wasn't warm or engaged either. Once I thought about, she never really embraced me. In my forty-eight years of life, she never once picked up the phone to call me. I never felt like she loved me and couldn't recall her ever saying she did.

Peewee and I talked a little while longer and he shared with me some experiences from his childhood that were eerily similar to mine. At that moment I begin to see him differently. For reasons I'm still not sure of, it helped me understand him a little more. Not a lot but a little. His experiences, although unfortunate, could not be used as an excuse for his absence for over forty years. When you know better, you do better. He had a chance even after prison to build a relationship with his children. His feeble attempt at it left broken men and women in its wake. Every child needs a father. They deserve it. Children need both parents. We were not created to exist separately. The family structure, as it was intended, is compromised when there is an absent parent, especially when that parents absence is because of his or her own doing. But today was a new day. I was seeking to walk and live in truth, love, and forgiveness. I wasn't angry with him or my mom and I told him so. Life is fleeting, and I had to live for the right now. I wanted no regrets.

As our call came to an end and we went through the pleasantries of saying our goodbyes, guess what? He said, "I love you sweetheart."

It wasn't the first time I heard him say it, but it was the first time he said it and I believed him. I told him that I loved him as well. He had been the father I had known for forty-eight years. How could I not? I sat in the car and cried that day for the loss of a father that I had never had.

Following our conversation he sent me a text. He thanked God for me and admired my strength. He thought that I was to be commended for how I was handling the situation. Again, he said he loved me. He said I would always be his "first," and again, I believed him.

I was free in that moment. No more secrets. No more lies.

CHAPTER NINE
F.L.O. FOR LADIES ONLY

"And they overcame him by the blood of the Lamb, and by the word of their testimony; and they loved not their lives unto death." Revelation 12:11

This chapter is dedicated to my Co-Pastor Susie C. Owens and Pastor Kristel Woodhouse, who had no idea that as they led a twelve-week bible study called For Ladies Only, F.L.O, I was working on rebuilding my life. How ironic was it that the class started on the same day that I found out about my biological dad, and that the second class would be the day that I would hear his voice for the first time? How Ironic was it that the class would focus on rebuilding? I went into this class not knowing what to expect but at the same time, I had high expectations. I was eager to see how it would all unfold. It would be my first time witnessing the mother and daughter duo serving in ministry together in such an intimate setting.

The first night we crowded the room. I was surprised at the huge turnout. It was literally standing room only. I couldn't help but scan the room and wonder at the many women present that had their own stories. How many daughters were there that night, daughters who had yet to discover their true identity? How many broken little girls were in the class with mommy issues? I knew I wasn't the only woman in the room who had discovered or unlocked doors that led to hidden truths. After the first night, the class was moved to the sanctuary. It was the only space in the building that could accommodate such a large audience of hungry women. We were hungry for the word of God.

Every Monday, the classes were all thought provoking and engaging. The book used as a study guide, *Growing Through Crisis* by Martha Tyler, focused on the story of Nehemiah, a cupbearer to King Artaxerxes and how he rebuilt the walls of Jerusalem. Nehemiah had heard about the walls of Jerusalem being in ruins while he was in his position as cupbearer to the king, and was moved with compassion to rebuild them. Nehemiah faced many obstacles from within the walls and without, but his passion kept him focused. The obstacles came from family and foes alike. Yet, he was determined to rebuild. In spite of the obstacles, Nehemiah was able to persuade the people to work together, and the walls were rebuilt in just fifty-two days. I would have thought that a women's bible study would focus on the usual suspects from the bible e.g., Sarah, Ruth, Esther or even Rahab, but not a man. God knew best and so, there we were, hundreds of women waiting to see how this story of a man named Nehemiah would somehow correlate with our own lives.

A cupbearer held a high but dangerous position in the kingdom. A cupbearer's job was to protect the king. A cupbearer had to make sure that the king wasn't being poisoned. The cupbearer placed his life on the line every day. He tasted the king's wine and food before it was served to the king. If there were any attempts to overthrow the king by way of poison, the cupbearer would be the one to take the hit. The cupbearer had to enter the royal courts wearing a certain countenance. The cupbearer had to appear happy at all times while in the presence of the king. It was a crime punishable by death to come before the king with a sad or depressed countenance. Oh how difficult this must have been! I couldn't imagine, every day reporting to a job and no matter what was going on in my everyday life, having to wear a smile.

As women, we often put our lives on the line for our families, friends and even our enemies. We walk around with smiles on our faces even when all hell is breaking loose in our lives. We've learned to smile through our tears. When misunderstood and taken for granted by family and friends, we smile and move on through life. We have mastered "fake it until you make it." Our countenance does not reflect what is on our hearts. How many times have we been in a room full of people laughing and smiling, only to go to bed that night and drown our pillows with tears?

Nehemiah had something that is worth striving to obtain. He had courage. He took the chance and went before the king with a sad countenance. He didn't try to hide what was on his heart. His heart was broken for his city and his people and he could no longer pretend that all was well. He went to the king and asked for permission to leave his position to go and see about his home. Nehemiah found favor with the king because of his courage. This favor allowed him to not only receive permission to go back to his homeland, Jerusalem and rebuild the walls, but the king also granted his request for help obtaining the tools and materials he would need from the surrounding neighbors.

Each week, I found myself somewhere in the lesson. I was putting the walls of my life back together brick by brick. I decided to stop pretending. All was not well. I had been broken and battered by life. I was so weary from trying to be all things to everybody that I had begun to suffer. I wasn't going to smile when I didn't want to. It was okay for me to say "no" to my family and friends. I had to unapologetically take care of Amy first. It was time for me to rebuild, reignite, recover and restore everything that the devil tried to steal from me. I had to take a chance and go before God without pretense. I got up the courage to go before Him believing that I would find favor.

First, I had to work on rebuilding my relationship with God. Too many times, I let the enemy come in and throw me off track. I lost my footing and I almost slipped, no I did slip. As a matter of fact, I slipped and a fell, more than once. How, when God is able to keep us from falling? I had to find out why it had been so easy for me to go back to my old life so many times. I realized that it was about me wanting acceptance. I needed to fit in. I wanted to belong to something. The acceptance started with my family. I didn't care about fitting in with groups, crowds and cliques. I wanted to fit in with my family. Feelings of rejection by my family were the root cause of me seeking dangerous attention elsewhere. I wanted my family to like me and accept me outside of what I could do for them. My walls were in ruins, but thanks to God for the mind to rebuild. Like Nehemiah, I took a survey of the mess that was around me and put together a plan to rebuild. I stopped enabling family members. They would have to love me for who I was and not for what I had or what I could do for them. I took a good look at my circle of friends. I only kept those around me who had a mind to rebuild with me. I started going to church even when I didn't feel like it. And yes, I am very much aware that my salvation is not predicated upon my church attendance, but I once heard a pastor say, *"How can a fish live outside of water?"* I purposely set out rebuilding relationships with those of a like mind. I was in such a mess at times, that I pushed away those who were praying for me and those who wanted to see me at my best in God. I didn't want "church" relationships. Yes, we *are* the Church (this is what we say when we want to make an excuse for not going to church), but we must not let the enemy isolate us and cause us to forsake the assembling of ourselves with the saints.

Secondly, I had to reignite the fire that had become just a flicker in my life. There was a time when I was on fire for God and the things of God. I was a missionary and took the title to heart. I had what some would call a street ministry. I would go out and compel the people to come to Christ. I witnessed on the same drug strips that I used to hang out on and I boldly talked to drug dealers about Jesus. I loved to brag about what the Lord had done in my life. For those that knew me prior to my getting saved, the transformation was obvious. During the height of my street ministry, I would visit friends who were not yet saved and preach the gospel to them. I would visit one of my childhood friends' house, and right at the time that she and her friends were ready to enjoy their libations for the evening, I would start talking about Jesus. One night, I talked so much that the sun came up and not one bottle of alcohol had been opened. This same friend found her way to the streets and became an addict. I prayed for her and compelled her to come to Jesus. I planted the seed. And guess what, that same friend has been free from drugs for over ten years. I was on fire for God, and then life happened and that fire began to diminish. I had become comfortable with being around *firefighters*. In class I learned the difference between *firefighters* and *firelighters*. *Firefighters* told me to stop doing so much. They said it didn't take all of that. They questioned where I was in God. They brought my sins before me. It was time for me to seek out the *firelighters* in my life. *Firelighters* encourage. They're the ones that pray for me and with me. They hold me accountable. They rebuke me when I'm stepping out of His will. They push me to get in God's presence. I thank God today for every rebuke that was given out of love. I thank God for the godly relationships that I have been blessed to build.

Thirdly, I had to recover. It was time to take back

everything that the devil tried to steal. It was time to recover all. The devil wanted me to believe that I would be trapped in the cycle of abuse. He wanted me to believe I was the part of my mother that I use to hate. I was an angry woman, I admit at one time, but the incessant curse of anger and bitterness within my family had to stop with me. I once believed the devil's lies. He told me I wasn't enough. I wasn't good enough, pretty enough, or smart enough. Nobody could love me because I wasn't lovable. I was too mean. I would never fit in. My family would never accept me for me. I wouldn't be a good wife or a good mother. I would always be drowning in dept. I would forever be the borrower and never the lender. I wouldn't finish school. Recently, he told me that I wouldn't have time to build a relationship with my biological dad, saying that time was not on our side.

Not only did I rebuke everything the devil told me, I started recovering my stuff. Daily I look in the mirror and affirm the woman looking back at me. I know who I am and I've stopped looking for validation from others. I no longer care about fitting in. I am who God created me to be, I am Amy. Instead of believing the lies from hell, I remind myself of all my accomplishments and every goal that I've met. I started paying my bills on time. I cut up credit cards that I didn't need. I gave myself credit for going back to college and finishing. In 2017, I received my Bachelor of Arts degree as a Communications major, after starting college twenty years prior. I am a licensed cosmetologist and an entrepreneur. I've been married to my husband for fourteen years and out of our union, I became a mother of twins at the age of thirty-nine. I broke the generational curse of being an unwed mother that had plagued my family for four generations. I broke the generational curse of abuse that had been in my bloodline for God knows how long. I recovered all.

And lastly, God restored. He restored my relationship with my mother. Every now and then we do a little song and dance when trying to express our feelings, but we've learned to communicate. We have a healthier relationship. We aren't afraid to say, "I'm sorry," and mean it. I love her for who she is and I love her where she is. I've accepted her love for me. I'm learning every day not to judge her. There are no strings attached to my love for my mother. I'm not holding her hostage to our past. 1 Peter 4:8 say's, "*Love covers a multitude of sins.*" I've been forgiven and she has too. God has given us each another chance. I wrote this book because of and for my mother. She told me years ago that there was a book in me. She had said to me on more than one occasion, "Don't let your book die in you." If you ever have a chance to witness us together, it's not an act. We aren't "performing" anymore. You get all of us. Our love and mutual respect for one another is as real as it gets. I like my mother and I am honored to be her daughter. When you enter my mom's home now, what are most noticeable are the pictures. Gone are the days of bare walls and mantles. Wherever there is space, there is a picture. There are pictures of me, pictures of my siblings, and pictures of her grandchildren. My favorite picture is one of my little sister and me; we couldn't have been more than five and three years old.

My trust in men has been restored. I trust my husband to lead our household, and I trust him as my husband to father our children. I trust him with my secrets and with my heart. I trust him because I trust God. I trust that God has blessed our union.

God has restored my mind. He has given me a "*peace that passes all understanding,*" Philippians 4:7. As long as I keep my mind on Him, I'm kept in perfect peace. God has added to my life since that first night of the F.L.O. class. Finding my biological father didn't subtract from what I had already, it added to it. God enlarged my territory. I have a huge family, blended yes, but family nonetheless. I have a wonderful husband, who has been my friend for over thirty years, two beautiful miracles, Logan and David and a bonus son Brandon. I have a total of six brothers and eight sisters. God has blessed me with three fathers. Where at one point in my life I had none, today I have three. I have my dad Marshall Mays, my dad James Perry, and my dad Howard "Peewee" White. All three of these men love me in their own way and I love them. I don't have horror stories about my in-laws as other may have. Mine are the best. My sister in-love, Angel, and my mother-in-love Deborah, have loved me since I was sixteen years old. They have always been the same and I thank God for blessing me with two of the most selfless women I've ever met. Best of all, I have my loving mother, Nancy Marie Smith and my two bonus moms, Juanita Perry and Florence Mays. God did that! He did a new thing. He gave me more than enough. He restored my faith. I declare I am a blessed and highly favored woman! God reminded me that not only was time on my side, but He was going to restore the years that my biological father and I had lost. Every day of the forty-eight years, where the devil thought he had won, God has promised to restore.

It's taken many years of searching but I've found Amy. I found her in my mother. I found her in my children. I found her in my mistakes. I found her searching for Sarah and Kate Carter. I found her in Peewee and I found her in James. I found her when I found Marshall. She was always there. All I had to do was look. She was there from birth. She was in every tragedy and in every triumph. I didn't need to be anyone other than who God had created me to be. Every crisis in my life unveiled another part of who I was. Without those crises, I may not have even had the guts to search for Sarah and Kate, let alone search for me. I grew through crises. I have proven to be tougher and stronger than I ever thought. Many have thrown in the towel that had gone through far less than I, but I am a survivor. I am rebuilder.

If you've ever experienced the pain and sorrow of not knowing your father, having an absent father, losing a father, or maybe you have had the same experience as me, don't be dismayed. Nothing can stop the plan of God for your life. Whatever you are going through, don't lose yourself and don't lose your hope. If you feel as if you've lost yourself, stop what you're doing and begin the journey of finding yourself by first giving your life to Jesus.

Confess Jesus with your mouth and believe in your heart that God has raised him from the dead. Secondly, find some firelighters to help ignite your fire. Thirdly, pray and when you are finished, pray some more. And finally, don't give up on God because He won't give up on you. Remember, it's never too late to start or start over. In the words of my daddy, Pastor Marshall Darnell Mays, "Don't die on Patmos." Don't allow the enemy to run you to a place of isolation. The Isle of Patmos is not your final resting place. Decide to live. You were created to live. I've decided to live, and in living I would like to reintroduce myself:

"Hi, my name is Amy. Amy Nichelle Mays Smith Langley. I am the proud daughter of Nancy Marie Smith Crawford and Marshall Darnell Mays. I am a wife and a mother. I am a descendant of Sarah and Kate Carter. I am a child of the only true and living God."

Scriptures that got me through this writing process:

"The end of a matter is better than it's beginning…" Ecclesiastes 7:8

"Agree with God, and be a peace; thereby good will come to you" Job 22:21

"Brothers and sisters, if someone is caught in a sin, you who live by the Spirit should restore that person gently. But watch yourselves, or you may also be tempted." Galatians 6:1

"Above all, love each other deeply, because love covers a multitude of sins." 1 Peter 4:8

Amy Langley

Made in the USA
Coppell, TX
06 December 2020

43215483R00080